The Time for Endowment
Building Is Now

The Time for Endowment Building Is Now

Why and How to Secure Your Organization's Future

Deborah Kaplan Polivy

ROWMAN & LITTLEFIELD
Lanham • Boulder • New York • London

Published by Rowman & Littlefield
An imprint of The Rowman & Littlefield Publishing Group, Inc.
4501 Forbes Boulevard, Suite 200, Lanham, Maryland 20706
www.rowman.com

6 Tinworth Street, London SE11 5AL, United Kingdom

British Library Cataloguing in Publication Information Available

Library of Congress Cataloging-in-Publication Data

Names: Polivy, Deborah Kaplan, 1947– author.
Title: The time for endowment building is now : why and how to secure your organization's future / Deborah Kaplan Polivy.
Description: Lanham : Rowman & Littlefield, [2021] | Includes bibliographical references and index. | Summary: "Here's a concise, easy-to-understand guide to the objective of the philanthropic gift. This book emphasizes endowment building and eliminates the confusion built into the terms 'gift planning,' 'legacy giving,' and 'planned giving.' It focuses on the ultimate goal of the gift—to build the endowment of the respective not for profit organization."—Provided by publisher.
Identifiers: LCCN 2020031173 (print) | LCCN 2020031174 (ebook) | ISBN 9781538137888 (cloth) | ISBN 9781538137895 (epub)
Subjects: LCSH: Endowments. | Nonprofit organizations.
Classification: LCC HV25 .P59 2021 (print) | LCC HV25 (ebook) | DDC 658.15/224—dc23
LC record available at https://lccn.loc.gov/2020031173
LC ebook record available at https://lccn.loc.gov/2020031174

∞ ™ The paper used in this publication meets the minimum requirements of American National Standard for Information Sciences Permanence of Paper for Printed Library Materials, ANSI/NISO Z39.48-1992.

For Gideon Abraham Tamuz
It's your turn!

Contents

Preface

The Time for Endowment Fundraising Really Is Now

Baby Boomers to advertisers: We've got the money.[1]

When I proposed this book, I was primarily concerned with why so many not-for-profit organizations do *not* actively pursue endowment contributions. Since then, which really is not so long ago, I have become increasingly compelled to write about the reasons they *should* engage in endowment building. These include the impact of the 2017 Tax Act on charitable giving and the impending and even current transfer of wealth by baby boomers. Some of this latter money could be captured by not-for-profit organizations were they to mobilize themselves to obtain it. Or, said another way, it is essential that charitable institutions pay attention to the wealth transfer and vigorously seek endowment gifts, and for many of those who have mature endowment funds, it is time to upgrade their endowment fundraising processes, procedures, and, most important, policies.

I have always been an advocate of endowment fundraising; it is necessary for the future vitality of small and mid-size charitable organizations. Even some veteran institutions that have sizable endowment funds need to take a look at the way in which they raise and use endowment monies if they, too, want to remain healthy over time. And yet so many organizations are just not paying attention to how they pursue endowment gifts, if in fact they even do, and to how they use the donations they receive especially in relation to unrestricted future contributions.

Organizations often do not actively pursue endowment gifts and/or think about how they ultimately expend them because their leadership is primarily concerned with meeting annual budgets. In addition, those organizations that are not seeking endowment donations, especially the small to medium-size ones, frequently do not do so because their leaders think that this kind of fundraising is expensive and difficult especially because of the language that is commonly associated with it—"planned giving"—which is perceived as complicated. While these reasons are important impediments to endowment building, the time has come to overcome them and vigorously proceed with this effort.

The data on the impact of the 2017 Tax Act on charitable giving are still somewhat inconclusive except in relation to those people whose contributions were influenced by their ability to obtain income tax deductions.[2] In an interview with the *PBS News Hour*, Stacy Palmer, editor of *The Chronicle of Philanthropy*, reported that "charities, especially small, mid-size groups, say they're feeling the pain [of the Tax Act] more than big organizations. And part of this is because people who are fairly wealthy can still itemize and get that tax deduction. But most middle-class to middle-class, affluent people, those are the people who lost that deduction. And they're the ones who don't have any incentive to give because of taxes."[3] The assumption in her statement is that these "middle-class to middle-class, affluent people" are the ones most likely to support small and mid-size organizations. And while Palmer admits that the tax deduction may not be the only reason that some of these individuals reduced the size of their traditional contributions, she continues, "There are estimates that as much as $20 billion might have been lost to charities in a year because of this tax change." In spite of these numbers, she reminds us that people "are still giving."[4]

These "middle-class to middle-class, affluent people" that Palmer cites include many of those baby boomers who will provide the "greatest wealth transfer in U.S. history." It is "estimated that $59 trillion will be transferred from 93.6 million American estates between 2007 and 2061."[5]

The authors of the Boston College report from which these numbers come, "A Golden Age of Philanthropy Still Beckons: National Wealth Transfer and Potential for Philanthropy Technical Report," conclude that a portion of these monies will be contributed to not-for-profit organizations if "fundraisers and charitable causes continue their current level of effort to obtain charitable donations and bequests." However, they state, "if their approach to fundraising becomes more effective, they have an opportunity to increase the amount that goes to charity well above our estimates."[6] In other words, there is a huge potential to raise endowment funds from the baby boomer generation—those born between 1946 to 1964[7]—and especially the people at the older end of this age range. So, while my initial thought was to focus this book primarily on doing away with the impediments to endowment development, and it still is, the reasons to do so are incredibly compelling.

In spite of the necessity to mobilize ourselves to "up the ante" in the not-for-profit sector and invest some major resources in raising endowment monies, this subject is totally ignored in a several-page article in *The Chronicle of Philanthropy* entitled, "Can the Boom Times Last?" While the piece suggests countless ways to ensure that "uncertainty" about future giving is addressed through a list of fundraising techniques, it makes no mention of endowment building. It promotes such approaches as focusing on the "biggest donors," technology, donor designation, "mail appeals tailored to specific midlevel donors," "peer-to-peer fundraising," identification of "small, highly motivated niches of supporters and appeal[s] to their interests directly," "targeted ads," and "corporate partnerships." Endowment building is addressed tangentially at best by noting that some successful, large campaigns had obtained "planned-gift pledges."[8]

In other words, in spite of the very unique circumstances that we are living in, if this article from November 2019 in *The Chronicle of Philanthropy* is an example of current thinking in relation to endowment development, then the latter is not getting the attention it should nor that the authors of the Boston College report suggest. This is not to say that articles have not been published about building endowment funds. They have been and continue to be. However, their writers use the terminology of "planned giving" and/or focus on the creation of bequest programs. Neither of these is suitable to capture the amount of money that could be available if we were to widen our lens and change our language.

This book addresses these issues. The first part describes endowment development and how the complexity of the vernacular often gets in the way of pursuing the function especially on the part of those organizations that probably need it the most to survive. This is especially true if annual giving declines because of a changing economy and tax situation. In this section, I also describe the lack of consistency and often transparency across the not-for-profit sector in terms of how endowment gifts are handled especially in relation to realized, unrestricted contributions that primarily result from bequests or charitable gift annuities and trusts. I also ask a question that other people have thought about, too. Should we even be putting money away for the future since we have so many societal problems that could benefit from contributions today? In other words, is annual giving "the way to go" and the contemporary imperative?

The next section of the book is a case study about the Harold Grinspoon Foundation's Life & Legacy Program, which is national in scope but local in implementation. I have included it for two reasons. First, Life & Legacy provides a model that other funders, whether community or private foundations, corporations, or a combination of these, could follow if they recognized that endowment development is essential to the health of the not-for-profit sector in which they operate. Second, the language, strategy, and goal of Life & Legacy are all very clear. The intent of the program is to both encourage and help local community-based charitable organizations build endowment funds using incentives and intense training. Words like "planned giving" do not appear in the Grinspoon program materials.

The last part of the book will describe how to design and build a good endowment program without complexity. It starts with chapter 5, "Who Are Endowment Donors?" which is especially worth reading if only to do away with the concentration on and sometimes obsession with the most wealthy that dominate fundraising in the not-for-profit sector.

Chapter 6, "Welcome to the Office of the Chief Legacy Officer," once again addresses the issue of language and how it is confusing in relation to endowment building. In this chapter, the focus is on not only the various titles assumed by professional staff but, maybe more importantly, the incongruity of the labels attached to fundraising departments as a whole. What is an Office of Institutional Advancement and how does a donor know what that name means? As philanthropy leader Simone Joyaux says, so many of the words that we use in fundraising are inappropriate to the function. "Vocabulary matters," she claims, and she is correct.[9]

While some of the most common and easy-to-use types of endowment giving techniques, such as charitable gift annuities or outright IRA designations, are described in chapter 7, "It's Not All About Bequests," it is only in the context of their benefits for donors and the organizations using them. The specific tools for endowment building that I describe in this chapter share a common characteristic in that no attorney or other professional adviser is required for their execution. Paperwork is limited to the donor and the not-for-profit organization receiving the gift, and as a result, costs and complications are few. I also include donor-advised funds in this chapter because, under the right circumstances, they, too, can be used as an instrument for endowment building and they, like the other vehicles that I include, do not need any professional adviser to draft documents to establish a fund. Outright endowment contributions are also included because they, too, are a simple gift-giving option. Fundraisers often overlook these or sometimes categorize them as "major gifts." It really does not matter how they are labelled as long as donors are introduced to them as a mechanism for establishing an endowment fund.

Chapter 8, "How to Build an Endowment Program," describes not only the role of the CEO and volunteer decision makers, the board, in supporting the creation of endowment building in an organization, but in particular their responsibility, as Doug White, a well-known expert in this field, says, "to give the process a lot more granular thought to this than most do."[10] Organizational leadership needs to challenge itself by reviewing, or if they do not exist, creating, endowment development policies and procedures and evaluating whether they "work" in relation to ensuring the future health of the respective institution. This chapter explains that often traditional ways of operating impede endowment building instead of encouraging it. This chapter also addresses marketing and the role of professional advisers in both launching a program and ensuring its success.

The final chapter of the book summarizes my conclusions and proposes future research, all of which result from the material that I present. While so many people have told me that donors do not care how their future gifts are used by an organization, I think we need to know if this is in fact true. We must conduct some formal research to test that notion. We also have to be very clear that boards of directors or trustees, however they are called, are responsible for ensuring that endowment building is ongoing; it is not stopped because of the challenges of the annual campaign, leadership turn-over, or whatever other short-term issues might arise. Doug White says it well: board members are the "caretakers" of not-for-profit organizations; "they are responsible" for an institution's "present *and* its future" (emphasis in the original).[11] This final chapter emphasizes the importance of their role.

I do not discuss the topics of tax deductions or other legal and accounting intricacies that are related to endowment donations because there are a multi-tude of resources that do so. Endowment investment and management are also topics that are addressed by experts more astute than I, although it is essential that these two functions are included in any endowment develop-ment plan and many state laws require attention to these practices. Moreover, from time to time, donors will ask, at least when making an initial contribu-tion, how their monies will be invested and distributed, and the person clos-ing the gift must either know the answer to that question or how to obtain it. While bequests are frequently referred to in the book, they, like other com-mon gift-giving techniques, are described extensively and exhaustively in other publications.

The primary purpose of this book is to demonstrate that it is imperative that all organizations review the way in which they are raising—or not—endowment monies, especially given the current financial environment in which we are living. If the not-for-profit sector does not mobilize to address this challenge, then all of us and especially the next generation will suffer.

Another purpose of the book is to show that endowment development is a complementary undertaking within the fundraising enterprise and that con-fusing and unclear terminology and esoteric approaches that compartmental-ize the function will result in a loss of funds. Leadership of large institutions such as hospitals and universities might find some interesting information that is new to them and/or causes them to adjust or even change some specif-ic aspects of their endowment-building policies as well as approaches to donors.

One of the most compelling issues for concern is how all organizations, no matter the size, dispose of the deferred gifts that they receive when there is no specific designation by the donor that they be placed in a permanent endowment fund. This is an important issue that I address in many different ways throughout the book because I worry that if organizations do not deposit these contributions into such a repository, they could be cannibalizing their own efforts.

This book will be helpful to executive staff and board members who are considering the establishment of an endowment program. It describes what needs to be in place in order to ensure that donors and, when appropriate, their professional advisers have confidence that whatever endowment gift is ultimately made will be properly managed and spent according to the contributor's wishes. The book is also intended for those who have an endowment-building process in place but want a "checkup" to make sure it is in good shape or to see whether there is something that is amiss or maybe needs review, upgrading, or change.

As noted above, the book will also be of interest to veterans in the field who may not have thought about some of the issues discussed herein or who have considered and then dismissed them as not worthy of the effort to make change. In other words, the time has come for rethinking policies and procedures in relation to endowment building even in those organizations that have long histories in this arena.

In order to write the book, I have depended on examples from many not-for-profit organizations, my own personal experience, and interviews with experts and veterans in the field as well as Internet searches. My references are in no way exhaustive. The sector is just too large.

I hope this book catapults leaders of charitable organizations to seriously think about the timeliness of endowment development for the future of their institutions and to not be intimidated by those who say that it is "too complicated" or needs a huge investment of resources. It is not and does not. We all have a responsibility to ensure that the next generation of citizenry can take advantage of the same or similar level of service delivery from nonprofit organizations that is available to us and that we also have come to expect.

NOTES

1. Janet Morrissey, "Baby Boomers To Advertisers: We've Got the Money," *The New York Times*, October 16, 2017, B6.
2. Because of the COVID-19 pandemic, non-itemizers will have the opportunity to itemize in 2020 according to the Coronavirus Aid, Relief, and Economic Security Act, or CARES Act. Whether this will have any impact on actual donations is as yet unknown. However, in the long term, since this opportunity is only available for one year at the time of writing this book, it may have no appreciable impact on the amount of money that is donated to not-for-profit organizations. See https://info.pgcalc.com/cares-act.
3. *PBS News Hour*, "Is 2017 tax law responsible for declining share of U.S. charitable donors?" December 31, 2019.
4. *PBS News Hour*, "Is 2017 tax law responsible?"
5. PND (Philanthropy News Digest), "Wealth Transfer to Boost Charitable Giving Through 2061, Study Finds," May 29, 2014.

6. John J. Havens and Paul G. Schervish, "A Golden Age of Philanthropy Still Beckons: National Wealth Transfer and Potential for Philanthropy Technical Report," Center on Wealth and Philanthropy, Boston College, May 28, 2014, 6.

7. Merriam-Webster, "Definition of Baby Boomer," https://www.merriam-webster.com/dictionary/baby%20boomer.

8. Eden Stiffman and Emily Haynes, "Can the Boom Times Last?" *The Chronicle of Philanthropy*, November, 2019, 8.

9. Simone P. Joyaux, "Fund Raising Vocabulary: Words I Hate," Charity Channel, https://charitychannel.com/fundraising-vocabulary-words-i-hate/?fl_builder&print=print.

10. Douglas E. White, e-mail to author, March 18, 2010.

11. Douglas E. White, *The Art of Planned Giving* (New York: John Wiley & Sons, 1995), 226.

Acknowledgments

I thank the leaders of the Harold Grinspoon Foundation including Harold himself and Winnie Sandler Grinspoon, president, for permitting me to use its Life & Legacy program as a case study for this book. Arlene D. Schiff, national director of Life & Legacy, was incredibly supportive, and not only did she answer all of my questions, but she did so without hesitation and with great speed. I could not have written about Life & Legacy without her, and I am so grateful not only for her cooperation but also for her generosity with her time and attention.

Once again I relied on Lisa Gurwitch, president and chief executive officer at Delivering Good, Inc., to critique my manuscript, and as with my prior books, she did a yeoman's job. She always provides a critical eye and incisive comments. Lisa, I deleted almost all of the words "I think" and "I believe"!

Amy Goldman, senior director at MIT's Office of Gift Planning, also offered insightful observations. She replied to my numerous questions with wit and speed.

Hannah Berger and Steven Meyers read the manuscript and provided valuable perspectives, too. I constantly ask Steven for advice, and he never hesitates to push me to think about an issue way beyond what I might have accomplished on my own.

There were so many other people who helped me with this book. I repeatedly called on Angela Powers and Cathrine Fischer Schwartz. Each time they responded graciously, and their comments were always constructive. It is wonderful to have colleagues who are also friends and who are willing to generously share their impressive knowledge about and experience in the field of fund development.

Charles S. Glassenberg, David Chused, Linda Mazur, Joe Imberman, Neal Myerberg, Stacy Sulman, Mark Jones, Lawrence Henze, Jennifer Weinstock, Douglas E. White, Ted Zablotsky, Sharleen Wallach, Greg Lassonde, Matthew C. Levin, Beth Appelman, Jacob Schreiber, Olga Tarasov, Morgan Schwartz, and Jeffrey Solomon graciously responded when I called upon them—often more than once.

I also want to thank Charles Harmon, executive editor at Rowman & Littlefield Publishers. He was enthusiastic about my book proposal from the time I submitted it, and he allowed me the flexibility in writing that I so appreciated, although he regularly checked in to ensure that I would reach the finish line. His editorial associate, Erinn Slanina, always had the appropriate answer to all of my questions. I also would like to thank production editor Lara Hahn, who ensured that this book was actually published. Thank you, Charles, Erinn, and Lara.

My husband, Richard, provided terrific support throughout this project. His proofreading has improved over the years, and I am most appreciative of his excellent comments and ongoing encouragement. Thank you, my dear.

Chapter One

Let's Call It What It Is: Endowment Development

In order to provide donors with the most varied opportunities to participate philanthropically with an organization, endowment options need to be a part of almost all fundraising efforts. Admittedly, they probably do not belong in new not-for-profits that have not had time to build up a cadre of loyal donors or in those with a limited life expectancy.

The first step in adopting a new endowment program or improving one already in existence is to eliminate obfuscating language that often scares and/or confuses fundraisers, board members, and donors alike. The most common term that fits this description is "planned giving." This phrase never made sense to me throughout my career, and not only did I try not to use it, but I always suggested to my consulting clients, potential donors, and students to avoid this phrase altogether and use another term such as "endowment building." My premise about the confusion the words "planned giving" conveyed became clear to me as a result of the following incident.

I was conducting a workshop for a well-established not-for-profit organization. Executive staff of the agency, development directors for individual component programs, as well as board members were all in attendance, and I was thrilled because everyone would hear the same message and it would not need to be communicated in a secondhand fashion to decision makers. (How many times do we as fundraisers go to a workshop that executive staff and board members do not attend? Then we have to describe what we learned, and, of course, since these decision makers were not present, they don't understand what we are trying to convey and certainly have no interest in making change.) The participants were deservedly proud of the history and longevity of their organization and its many projects, but there had never been a formal endowment development program, notwithstanding that so many of the donors were quite elderly and had been contributing for years.

In my presentation, I explained that a model donor's journey with an organization extends from his or her first gift to an "ultimate" or endowment contribution. One participant commented that leadership had been thinking of starting a limited endowment effort where bequests would be encouraged. She explained that "planned giving" was far too complex for the group.

No one mentioned outright endowment contributions or asking for different kinds of deferred donations, such as retirement fund designations. These are easy to administer and could have been used to ensure that the many programs and buildings that had been established over the years were maintained for the future. I realized immediately that this was an institution "ripe" for endowment building but that the board and staff were "frozen" by what they felt was too sophisticated an initiative for them—what they referred to as "planned giving." I recognized that with some basic training in listening to donors' stories, matching intentions with organizational needs, and determining the right kind of gift—present or future, income producing or not—they could turn around the entire fundraising enterprise and raise a lot more money over time. But there was really no interest on their part.

"Planned giving" refers to a group of tools or mechanisms, such as bequests or charitable gift annuities, by which an individual can make a future gift to an organization without giving up the use of either current assets and/or income. Why don't we just say that, especially when talking to donors?

"Planned giving" is the terminology that was adopted for deferred contributions, and historically, there was an assumption that once these donations were realized, the monies would be deposited in a permanent endowment fund. When I began in the field many years ago, we used the words "endowment development" to describe what we did.[1] In my mind, that is a much clearer phrase than the multitude of different terms that are used today.

There is no consistency in the fundraising field for what professionals in this arena—endowment development—do or are even called; some are legacy officers, donor advisers, donor engagement officers, gift planners, planned and major gift officers, and more. But as Amy Goldman, senior director of gift planning at Massachusetts Institute of Technology, claims, "I think the terminology of planned giving/gift planning has been around for so long now that people broadly have an understanding of what it means (though it means different things for different people . . . certainly with different outcomes)."[2] And so, if Amy is correct, there is really no uniform interpretation of what this language means nor expectation of results.

I think the term "planned giving" makes no sense since we all pretty much plan our charitable contributions whether for annual or capital campaigns or current and future endowment gifts. This perspective was clearly stated in probably the most popular book about planned giving, Debra Ashton's *The Complete Guide to Planned Giving*, published in 2004. She wrote, "A planned gift is any gift that combines conscientious decisions about how much to give, to whom to give and when to give it. As such, virtually all giving, from all people, at all times is planned giving. And the corollary: all development professionals are planned giving officers."[3] And yet, we make it appear that planned giving is something esoteric and beyond the capacity of ordinary human beings. We offer special courses about planned giving and pay high-priced consultants to train us in how to ask for and close these gifts.

There is another very important point suggested by the above quotation. By creating distinctive "planned giving" departments, programs, or even seminars specific to the subject, we place artificial separations between staff members—the opposite of what Ashton suggests. In effect, we create silos as opposed to introducing every fund development officer, board member, and executive staff person to the tools and techniques of endowment fundraising so that they can all feel comfortable participating in a meaningful conversation with a donor or prospect. As a result of the separations, we probably leave a lot of money "on the table" because we often overlook or are not even aware of the possibilities of a variety of gift-giving opportunities that we could discuss with donors if we knew how to do so. Through my own endowment development work, I realized how really easy it is to talk to supporters about alternatives to the annual campaign gift and even different forms of it wherein an outright endowment donation could fund a donor's ongoing annual contribution forever.

My first experience with such a donation occurred with an eighty-year-old widow. We noticed that her annual gift of $5,000 was made through an attorney who each year transferred shares of stock to our organization from a trust account in her name. I wondered whether we could obtain a one-time gift of $100,000 of appreciated securities, deposit them in our endowment, and then distribute $5,000 to the annual campaign every year on this woman's behalf. In this way, neither she nor the attorney would have to deal with the contribution in the future and her annual gift, hopefully, would last forever or at least over the lifespan of the organization. Moreover, we expected that due to good investment returns over time, the principal of the gift would increase and in turn the yearly distribution would also rise. (We recognized the opposite, too, but the long term was our focus.)

I contacted the attorney's office, and the next time he came to town to meet with this woman, I joined the conversation. Everyone was assured that we would be good custodians of the money, and the donor was thrilled that she would no longer be contacted and asked for an annual contribution. On the other hand, I did stay in touch with her and let her know when the distribution in her name was made to the campaign and visited her at least twice a year to keep her informed about our work. All involved—the donor and our organization as well as the attorney—were happy with the new arrangement. And this was definitely a gift that was planned; it took time to propose, consider, and execute, but it involved no deferred gift-giving tool or technique. It was an outright endowment contribution, something we often forget to talk about with potential donors because of a focus on planned and estate gifts. (See chapter 7, "It's Not All about Bequests," for more on this subject.)

My point is supported by a study conducted by Russell N. James III, who wanted to discern whether language had any effect on "understanding and interest in learning more regarding 'planned giving,' 'estate giving,' 'estate planning,' and 'charitable gift annuities.'" He concluded that "using these standard industry terms to introduce such information reduces both understanding and interest in learning more as compared with simple functional descriptions, such as 'other ways to give,' 'gifts in wills,' 'will planning,' and 'gifts that pay you income.'"[4] Similar words to these are used in the very successful Grinspoon Foundation's Life & Legacy Program described in chapter 4. James concludes that "although formal industry terminology may be technically correct, it can also be detrimental to client understanding and interest in learning more about such topics."[5]

Various charities are beginning to learn and act on this lesson. For example, according to an article in the March 2019 *Chronicle of Philanthropy*, "A Steady Pipeline of Bequests," Catholic Relief Services realized that it needed a "complete refresh of its planned-giving communications. Now the charity reaches out to donors with simpler text, more photos, and more stories from the field."[6] Interestingly, however, *The Chronicle of Philanthropy* continues to use the terminology "planned giving" when describing these and other such fundraising efforts. It may be, as one of my interviewees suggested, that its writers are more comfortable with the technical language, notwithstanding that different words may be more welcoming to donors, professionals, and other readers of its publication.

In comparison to the above example about Catholic Relief Services, another not-for-profit organization published an article in a membership newsletter with the title "New Planned-Giving Push Celebrates 70 for 70."[7] The casual reader who understands nothing about the term "planned giving" may not have proceeded to even peruse the piece. Moreover, it is not until the fourth paragraph that "examples of planned gifts" are actually identified—and these, too, are somewhat obtuse in name except for "bequests."

Why can't we just simply say that "in honor of our seventieth birthday, you can make a gift of cash or appreciated assets today and even obtain an income stream"? Or "you could establish an endowment fund bearing your name or the name of someone you love"? These words are easy to understand.

For those organizations that do move forward into endowment development, I have another major issue with terminology: the words "endowment campaign," which are an oxymoron. Endowment building is something that has no end; it continues throughout the lifespan of an institution and beyond because every organization should have instructions in its by-laws or other legal documents as to the ultimate depository of the permanent endowment in the event that the organization goes out of business entirely or merges with another not-for-profit. Moreover, even in the rare chance that an endowment ceases to receive new gifts, it is still invested for growth—or at least it should be. There is no end to endowment building.

Endowment fundraising cannot be a campaign by its very nature because donors make estate gifts in an ongoing way and the timing of their realization is an unknown. There is no finish to endowment building like there is to a campaign. The very premise upon which endowment development and spending is built is its continuity or, maybe better said, long-term horizon.

And yet notwithstanding this fact, I find job notices looking for fundraisers to oversee "endowment campaigns." For example, this one was posted on an Internet site: "Director of Planned Giving and Endowment Campaign: [name of organization] has an exciting opportunity for a talented fundraiser looking to strengthen Planned Giving and Endowment campaign efforts."[8]

Organizations often count "promises" of gifts in their so-called endowment campaigns, especially through bequests. Promises can be broken for any number of reasons, for example, change of heart or the lack of funds at end of life. Sometimes these promises are never actualized through a legal mechanism such as a signed or notarized will or trust document. This is why I am often called upon by organizations to discuss how to turn "promises" into reality by securing either current gifts in their place, documented future commitments, or, as Steven Meyers describes in his book, *Personalized Philanthropy: Crash the Fundraising Matrix*, some combination of an outright and future donation. These are referred to as "blended gifts"—part current and part future.[9]

The issue of planned giving and endowment development becomes even more problematic when we think about the concept of "major gifts." Is an outright endowment gift like the one from the eighty-year-old woman described above a planned gift, a major gift, or something else entirely, and in our current departmental infrastructure, where does it belong and how is it counted—by the one gift of stock to the endowment or every year as a result of the distributions to the annual campaign? In other words, is it counted twice? And maybe counting proceeds should not be the real measure of success—maybe there are other measures such as donor retention or the action steps that a fundraiser takes to close a gift.[10] This conundrum extends further because we read so often that the person who actually is instrumental in obtaining a bequest probably is not even on staff when the gift is realized. So who gets the credit?

Stacy Sulman, vice president for personalized philanthropy and legal affairs at the American Committee for the Weizmann Institute of Science, is addressing this issue in relation to the fundraisers with whom she works. She wants to encourage each of them to become part of a team that talks to donors about all kinds of gifts. But she recognizes that the people who bring in the contributions today want to obtain credit for them while those who secure nonbinding future commitments are typically not recognized in our current fundraising infrastructure. It is a challenge, she claims, "to motivate fundraisers to ask for revocable commitments that may not be realized for a long time. I am trying to address this issue by finding a way that they [fundraisers] can be acknowledged for working on gift planning." For example, maybe "if they obtain a commitment or letter of intent that is not legally binding, these officers will get credit. In this way the fundraiser can demonstrate that he or she has achieved something and can obtain recognition for it. On the other hand," she continued, "donors often don't want to tell us that they have made such a gift. Our CEO supports such an effort and we are concentrating on people who are between 70 and 85."[11] She fully understands the potential amount of money that this latter group of people could give to the charity were they addressed strategically and if the fundraisers who speak to them could be more motivated to close a gift notwithstanding when it might be ultimately received. On the other hand, she states that if these same fundraisers obtain a "binding pledge," establish "a charitable gift annuity or trust," or work on a gift that results in "a transfer of funds from an IRA, these are considered current gifts" and the fundraisers are recognized for them.[12]

Endowment development relates to building up assets, investing them, and spending a percentage over time. Planned giving, if we even use that term, connotes a number of tools through which endowment contributions can be made. Endowment development is an essential part of any overall fundraising effort, and it has three very real advantages—one for the donor and two for the not-for-profit organization that operates a well-managed program. First, for donors, endowment development adds to the variety of options from which they may choose when "planning" their charitable contributions over time. For the charitable organization, endowment development, when done well, allows gift officers to be creative and thus to thrive because they are not limited in terms of what they can discuss with prospects and contributors. Finally, the entire process ensures a stream of income for present and future institutional needs as well as emergencies should they occur.

Endowment development is not just about bequests, notwithstanding that many organizations market the latter to increase the former. In spite of this fact, some organizations that receive what are referred to as unrestricted bequests, those not designated by the donor specifically for the endowment, do not deposit the realized sums into their endowment funds. They use the monies as soon as they are received and/or place them into what is called a "quasi-endowment" or "board-directed endowment" from which they can take income and principal often according to policies and procedures. I find this behavior contradictory because endowment development as a function will never succeed if the organizations that on the one hand are trying to increase the number of bequests that they receive on the other hand are not placing the realized gifts into an endowment account and therefore investing them for the future health of the respective institution. I specifically address this issue in the next chapter.

We usually think of endowment fundraising as something that is for older people and usually the final step in a donor's journey with an organization. This viewpoint is emphasized in an article that appeared in *The Chronicle of Philanthropy*, "How to Strike Gold With Endowment Gifts,"[13] and it is increasingly relevant because of the predicted transfer of wealth that will occur in the next decade or so.

On the other hand, Steven L. Meyers "crashes" that notion with his book, *Personalized Philanthropy: Crash the Fundraising Matrix*, and I, like Steven, have raised endowment monies from people of all ages and income levels; although it is true that older people are probably the best prospects, there are others. (See chapter 5, "Who Are Endowment Donors?")

It is so important to understand that endowment donations provide another opportunity for an individual to contribute to an organization. It is not an effort that is put on a "back burner" because of the prominence or perceived importance of the annual campaign. It is a complementary fund development initiative that should be an integral component of an organization's total financial resource-generating effort. Or as Kay Sprinkel Grace, fundraising "guru," explains, by eliminating the concept of "annual" altogether, conversations with donors "can focus on multiple opportunities to contribute on an ongoing basis."[14] That is the ultimate objective of any fundraising program. This perspective also assumes the elimination of the concept of defining success according to annual receipts and the incorporation of wholly different measures, especially ones that focus on the growth of total monies from multiple sources over time. Steve Meyers introduces the notion of moving away from the "One Number"—the amount raised in any one year— to "counting and reporting gifts in a multidimensional, donor-focused way."[15]

Maybe this book will crash the "Planned Giving Complex" and introduce some ideas about endowment development that are more in line with the way in which donors, fundraisers, and not-for-profit leaders think about the future of the organizations about which they care. Despite the fact that everyone with whom I spoke in conducting research for this publication thought that the words "planned giving" were difficult to understand, sometimes misleading, technical in nature, "calcified,"[16] and certainly not interpreted similarly by all in the field, they continue to be used. Hopefully, through the chapters that follow, I clarify some of the ideas contained within the discipline of endowment building and bring it to a higher level of understanding for all who want to pursue its ultimate benefits.

NOTES

1. Steven Meyers agrees with me. When I asked him in an e-mail how he reacted to this sentence, he replied: "I think it is fair to say that your statement reflects a truth of how you (and I) were 'brung up' in fundraising and planned giving; it was all about endowment development." Steven Meyers, e-mail to author, April 26, 2020.

2. Amy Goldman, e-mail to author, January 2, 2020.

3. Debra Ashton, *The Complete Guide to Planned Giving* (Quincy, MA: Ashton Associates, 2004), ix.

4. Russell N. James III, "Creating Understanding and Interest in Charitable Financial and Estate Planning: An Experimental Test of Introductory Phrases," *Journal of Personal Finance* 17, no. 2 (Fall 2018): 9.

5. James, "Creating Understanding."

6. Heather Joslyn, "A Steady Pipeline of Bequests," *The Chronicle of Philanthropy*, March 2019, 19.

7. Brandeis University, "BNC's New Planned-Giving Push Celebrates 70 for 70," *Brandeis Magazine*, Winter 2018/2019.

8. Jewish Jobs, February 26, 2010, https://jewishjobs.com/jobs/view/55624.

9. Steven L. Meyers does a terrific job in describing alternative ways of making and counting gifts beyond simply present and future in his book, *Personalized Philanthropy: Crash the Fundraising Matrix* (Nashville: CharityChannel Press, 2015).

10. See my book, *The Donor Lifecycle Map: A Model for Fundraising Success* (Nashville: CharityChannel Press, 2017).

11. Stacy B. Sulman, interview with author, January 31, 2020.

12. Stacy B. Sulman, e-mail to author, March 19, 2020.

13. *The Chronicle of Philanthropy*, "How to Strike Gold With Endowment Gifts," December 2017, 38.

14. Kay Sprinkel Grace, *Beyond Fundraising*, 2nd ed. (Hoboken, NJ: John Wiley & Sons, 2005), 120.

15. Meyers, *Personalized Philanthropy*, xxii.

16. Douglas White, e-mail to author, March 18, 2020.

Chapter Two

What Is an Endowment Contribution?

I always assumed that all bequests and other realized deferred gifts automatically were deposited into a permanent endowment fund and managed according to the laws for investment and spending described in the Uniform Prudent Management of Institutional Funds Act, or UPMIFA.[1] This is what happened in the charitable organizations in which I had worked, and the purpose of the procedure was to build the value of the endowment over time and thus to also increase the spending power of the corpus. This practice was easy to both understand and implement. However, when I began consulting, I quickly learned that this was not how such contributions were universally handled.

For those of you who are not familiar with UPMIFA, it is a "complex law that holds sway in almost every state in the nation. It covers how charitable institutions are to administer donor-permanently-restricted gifts."[2] It only pertains to those donations where a donor states that he or she wants the contribution to be placed into a permanent endowment fund. A charity can do whatever it wants with any realized gift that has no such instruction attached to it, and what I learned over time is that they do.

When not-for-profit organizations receive an unrestricted bequest or other kind of what is often referred to as a planned or deferred gift with no instruction from the donor as to how the contribution should be treated, they regularly use the realized funds to defray current expenses, cover deficits, or put them into a board-restricted endowment that is not at all permanent in nature. Restricted or donor-designated gifts that are not specifically intended for the endowment are handled in much the same way except that they are directed to a purpose indicated by the contributor. Doug White, a well-known expert in this field, writes that even when there is a donor direction as to how a gift should be used, some "organizations, being budget-strapped, use the money

9

right off. This, even though a gift agreement might say otherwise, although even they are not all that specific."[3]

The way in which all of these realized deferred gifts—whether donor directed or otherwise—are spent becomes more complicated because there seems to be a varying understanding "of the use and application" of the words "permanent endowment fund." David Chused, assistant vice president of institutional advancement at Brandeis University, explained that there are multiple ways that "an endowment fund may be characterized or labelled" and these include "'permanent,' 'true,' 'quasi,' 'restricted,' 'temporarily restricted,' or 'unrestricted,' and in some cases these labels blur or may change over time." Chused also noted "that at any particular time the modifier that is used in tandem with the term endowment fund may vary depending upon the context in which the term is used, and perhaps more importantly, the individual who is invoking the term."[4] He continued, "A 'true' endowment fund is established only when a donor makes a gift and specifically directs, in writing, that the funds are to be invested in perpetuity."[5] To that there is universal agreement, notwithstanding White's comment above that donor-restricted gifts are sometimes not placed into a permanent endowment by the donee charity in spite of donor direction.

The question then becomes: does the donor know about this power of determination? And if he or she does not, do charitable organizations have the responsibility to communicate to the contributor that there are options for gift giving in terms of how the organization will ultimately use a contribution that is received sometime in the future? This is where the issue of endowment building becomes critical, in need of clarification and even increased transparency on the part of institutions seeking these contributions. One of the responsibilities of charities is to inform donors in as many ways as possible that they have a choice as to how their deferred gifts will be used.

In spite of this fact, there is still a lack of clarity in relation to the meaning of the word "endowment." The website of Columbia University uses two words—"true" and "permanent"—to describe endowment contributions: "A permanent ('true') endowment is a fund established in accordance with donor restrictions, to exist in perpetuity."[6] The United States Holocaust Museum introduces another word—"real"; it recommends to donors that they support the "Permanent Endowment Fund, an unrestricted permanent real endowment fund."[7] Chused does not include the word "real" in his list of descriptors. The issue is that the language related to endowment fundraising is not consistent across the board and maybe it "really" does not matter—or maybe it does from the perspective of the donor who is planning a gift through an estate.

The subject can become even more unclear as explained to me by Linda Mazur, senior director of trusts and estates at Pomona College. She stated that there are really two types of "restrictions." The first addresses "whether the gift will go into a current-use fund available to spend immediately or an endowed fund where the principal is preserved and only the income is spent. The second addresses the purpose the donor wants to support, such as scholarships or a particular department." According to Mazur, "A 'true' endowment is one restricted to endowment by the donor; otherwise it is an expendable gift. There can be a purpose restriction whether the gift is expendable or endowed."[8]

The Episcopal Church Foundation website pretty much matches Mazur's comments. It has a section entitled "Restricted vs. Unrestricted Endowments," under which there is a segment labeled "Definitions of 'True' (Restricted) and 'Quasi' (Unrestricted) Endowments." The website explains that "a 'true' or restricted endowment is established if a donor makes a gift to the Endowment Fund, often defining its use." If the church "receives gifts of any size for the Fund, those funds are equally restricted. If . . . donors give to an Endowment Fund for a named purpose, the funds are restricted as to purpose as well." The website continues that "if the church receives an unrestricted bequest, or receives funds from the sale of property . . . those funds are called a 'quasi' or unrestricted fund" and "can be spent down by the Vestry within established distribution rules."[9]

As far as the Episcopal Church Foundation is concerned, "the difference" between the two types of funds—quasi or permanent—is based on the instruction of the donor or lack thereof and how the "corpus" is preserved. The corpus, or "spending power of" what the church calls the "restricted endowment," is protected by the Uniform Prudent Management of Institutional Funds Act, or UPMIFA,[10] whereas the unrestricted or quasi-endowment "is protected by only whatever policies the church enacts."[11] Just to be a little more confusing, some organizations refer to the latter—the quasi-endowment—as a "Sustaining Endowment Fund."[12]

In comparison to the above, the San Diego Foundation does not use any of this language—true, quasi, or even sustaining—on its website. It states quite clearly that "an endowment is a permanent fund" whose monies "are pooled for maximum benefit and invested to achieve long-term capital growth. Contributions are irrevocable and become assets of the Foundation."[13] There is no other kind of fund referred to except "non-endowment funds," and they "have no permanent principal balance and are immediately available for grant distribution." These monies appear to be donor-advised funds (DAF) that provide the contributor with the ability to "make an immediate impact on the community" through the recommendation of allocations to not-for-profit organizations. These "funds are available for distribution the moment they are received by The . . . Foundation," and they have a "finite existence," as explained on the website. But "donors can transfer monies from the non-endowment fund to the endowment fund to help build a balance upon which gifts can be provided in perpetuity."[14] This seems to me to be the ultimate purpose of any community-foundation-based donor-advised fund program, and I would assume, hopefully correctly, that is why it is emphasized on this website. (For more about the role of DAFs in endowment building, see chapter 7—"It's Not All About Bequests.")

I think that all of these definitions can become very confusing for the donor and fundraiser alike. Some writers explicitly use the word "confusion" in the title of their articles—"Top 12 Points to Avoid Endowment Confusion"[15] or "Confusing Gift Terms."[16] Ellis Carter, author of the blog *Charity Lawyer: Nonprofit Law Simplified*, states that "in my practice I am often surprised by how little some fundraising professionals understand about the mechanics of gift restrictions—particularly the implications of permanent restrictions and legal meaning of the term 'endowment.'"[17]

The Fund Raising School at Indiana University's Lilly Family School of Philanthropy has distributed a 364-page (plus "updates") notebook to enrollees in its planned giving course, the ultimate purpose of which is to change the "mystery" associated with the subject of "planned gift" into "mastery."[18] Nothing in the "course objectives," however, is mentioned about the ultimate goal of cultivating planned gifts except, I assume, as another tool that fundraisers will have at their disposal.[19] There is a sentence in the foreword to the notebook that states, "Many charities with mature planned giving programs have experienced significant endowment growth thereby helping to ensure the organization's long-term financial viability."[20] And that's it until a brief section on "Endowments" where there is another reference; it is written that "Sources of Endowment" are "Outright and/or Planned Gifts" and "donors may consider funding endowment with both outright and planned gifts."[21] But there is no mention about the difference in the types of endowment funds. There is a statement in the notebook that one role of the Development Office is to determine from the donor the "ultimate designation or use of funds at termination of income beneficiaries' interests."[22]

And that is the issue. It is important that training about endowment development, especially if it is linked to planned giving, not only addresses the subject of donor determination of where a gift will ultimately be placed, but more importantly, that the difference in endowment funds be explicitly explained so that practitioners are in turn knowledgeable when talking to donors about their respective choices.

I have learned from research for this book about legal issues as well as differences in how endowment gifts are managed and spent, and yet, in all of the material that I have read that relates to gift planning and planned giving, there is little mention of the distinctions in the different kinds of endowment funds and how they affect the design of the gift. In other words, while the authors describe the tools, they make few or any references to their ultimate purpose except as serving as gift-giving vehicles. While all of this information has been created for the purpose of teaching about planned giving—the "tools of the trade," so to speak—there is little if any mention about *why* it is important to know about them, which I think is not only the most significant factor but is in fact endowment development—and in particular, the permanent endowment.

The explanation for this reality may be that there is no overall agreement that the results of these gifts are ultimately for the purpose of building the so-called permanent endowment. On the other hand, there is clearly the suggestion in the literature that the latter is the ultimate depository as noted in the foreword and short section in the planned giving notebook prepared by the Lilly School. But they are neither plainly nor directly linked nor is there any mention of the word "permanent" or otherwise.

Adrian Sargeant and Jen Shang take a similar stance in the chapter that they write on planned giving in their book, *Fundraising Principles and Practice*. They state that "by the end of this chapter you [the reader] should be able to:

1. Define planned giving
2. Describe the operation of a range of planned giving vehicles
3. Describe donor motivation for offering planned gifts
4. Explain how nonprofits currently solicit planned gifts
5. Describe the role of stewardship and recognition in facilitating planned gifts
6. Describe the role of the board in soliciting planned gifts."[23]

But there is no mention of the purpose or the *why* for a planned gift. What is its ultimate utility for the organization? What happens to the planned gift once the institution receives it? What does the latter do with it? And how does the design of the gift impact that decision?

There are two sentences in this planned giving chapter that even suggest that endowment building may be the ultimate goal of planned gifts: "Planned giving can also appeal to the wealthy, because they tend to be comfortable and familiar with the notions of long-term capital investment and endowment,"[24] and "capital rather than cash flow is the aim of planned giving programs, with nonprofits seeking to build the value of their endowments."[25] This latter sentence is at the end of the chapter as opposed to something that might appear at the very beginning in order to describe the purpose of undertaking the planned-giving effort in the first place. No rationale is ever mentioned except to say that "a planned gift is created now for the future benefit of a non-profit organization."[26] But is the "future benefit" spending when realized, investing in a permanent endowment, or something in between—the quasi-endowment? In this publication, too, planned giving seems to be included as another method for raising funds, and the link to endowment development is weak at best.

In order to make the disposition of future gifts clear and understandable by all involved, including professional advisers who draft testamentary and trust documents, there has to be a clear understanding of the difference in what are referred to as endowment gifts. Second, boards as well as executive leadership need to address the issue in order to communicate not only to donors but also to fund development staff the preferred repository of contributions that result from estate planning. And these same leaders need to grapple with their long-term vision for the organizations which they serve in order to state their preference for permanent endowment gifts if those are their choice. The rationale for this decision-making must be clear and communicated to current and potential donors. And then they can, after understanding the preferences of the organizations that they support, choose the repository that most coincides with their ultimate goals—a permanent, named endowment fund or something else entirely.

There are countless examples on the Internet of by-laws directing the ultimate use of these future gifts, and often they include descriptions about the roles of endowment committees in relation to appointment of participants, meetings, as well as design of investment and spending policies.[27] Moreover, while the Uniform Prudent Management of Institutional Funds Act, or UPMIFA, "only applies to funds given to a charity by a donor who has specified that the funds be permanently restricted," it "does not apply to charitable trusts or donor advised funds. It also does not apply to endowment funds established by a charitable institution itself from previously unrestricted funds."[28] In other words, the Act is very specific about gifts restricted by a donor for the endowment, but organizations have leeway to create their own policies in relation to other realized, unrestricted deferred gifts, and I suggest that they do so to ensure clarity for everyone involved. I propose that if these gifts are not permanently restricted by the donor, that at the minimum they be placed into a quasi-endowment with strict rules for investing and spending assets that mirror the permanent endowment.

Steven Meyers disagrees with me in relation to this recommendation. He writes,

> I've seen unrestricted gifts used for scholarships and research funds which are endowed, and I've also seen funds used for a project that needs cash for starting up something like new laboratories. A realized unrestricted gift will always be viewed as an opportunity to direct funds where they are most needed, and that may depend on how and when [they are] received and what commitments the charity wants to fulfill in a timely manner. Some charities— thinking ahead—have a policy that "results of planned gifts" should go into an endowment-like fund, as designated by the board. That is a great idea, but there is no reason to automatically direct the money into an endowment if the donor has not required it.[29]

However, he says, a board could establish "a 'quasi-endowment.' You get the most bang for the buck if you set up a quasi-endowment or 'board designated endowment' that is available for emergencies and 'make it inconvenient' to use by requiring 3/4 or 2/3 of a board vote to take out money beyond whatever spending rate is agreed upon."[30] His differentiation in relation to choice as to how these gifts are deployed should be a part of a board's policy as opposed to last-minute decision-making determined when the gift is received. Another issue related to Steven's comments is that money can get used up very quickly whatever option (or neither of which) is chosen, notwithstanding in the second option that "inconvenience" is built in.

If an organization's leadership decides to purposively accept the responsibility to build the permanent endowment, then it has to ensure that its communications to donors state this fact. It has to let contributors know that this is a priority and explain why. Charities have the responsibility, wherever and whenever possible, to educate prospects and donors about their respective choices in terms of making these gifts.

Not-for-profit organizations need to make a statement that endowment building is a priority, especially the permanent endowment, and if such a principle is not cogently weighed and established, then any initiative to build the endowment might be undermined by the institution itself. Moreover, since endowment funds take an extended time to grow, the effort should be assumed with the understanding that it is a "long-term project."[31]

After this determination is made, then a by-law should be created describing how future gifts that are not designated by a donor for the endowment will be used. There must be an intent on the part of the board and executive staff to encourage the growth or, in some cases, even the establishment of an endowment fund and obviously this needs to be a precursor to any by-law. In addition, there must be a clear understanding of the UPMIFA by a board so that it can cogently make the choices described in this book. On the other hand, as so many people have reminded me, while a board can make a by-law to establish a quasi-endowment that mimics the permanent in terms of investment and spending, a board can also make a by-law that modifies one that is currently in place given whatever rules for change are established by the board itself.

There are some organizations that are very clear about endowment building. For example, the Combined Jewish Philanthropies of Greater Boston passed a by-law in the "late 1960s" for exactly this purpose. It reads: "The following assets shall be included in the Endowment Fund for the Corporation: All gifts to the Corporation or its predecessors, whether testamentary or otherwise, (except sums expressly contributed for current operating purposes without other restrictions or to the annual campaign) which (i) are restricted in purpose or (ii) equal or exceed $1,000 and are unrestricted in purpose or use."[32] Since these gifts are not all determined by a donor to be deposited into a permanent endowment, the board has the right to make "additional distributions as community needs warrant" from these contributions notwithstanding that they are invested along with the permanent endowment.[33] This latter directive does not apply to the permanent endowment, which is made up of donor-designated contributions. However, at least in this case, the board is clear that it wants to build up the endowment and only spend the so-called quasi-endowment in extraordinary circumstances.

Greg Lassonde, in his course on legacy giving at the Sanford Institute of Philanthropy at John F. Kennedy University in Pleasant Hill, California, and in his consultancy practice, recommends a generic by-law that is based on the assumption that permanent endowment building is the goal. While he does not recommend "that all organizations create an endowment," he does "believe it's appropriate for the vast majority,"[34] and he proposes the following language: "whereas xyz agency wishes to institutionalize and expand its legacy giving program in order to build endowment over the coming years to further strengthen the organization." Notwithstanding this guidance, he then suggests the following verbiage for those organizations that want to adhere to a policy closer to what Meyers recommends above: "All unrestricted legacy gifts will be placed into endowment where they will be co-mingled with restricted gifts for investment purposes; at the Executive Director's discretion, up to 10% of the total annual value of all unrestricted gifts, to a maximum of $100,000, may be directed to the annual fund."[35] Model language varies widely.

Since organizations deploy their realized deferred gifts differently, it is really not at all certain that donors understand how their future contributions will be used especially in relation to bequests. So while writers about planned giving state that "planned gifts are essential to building the organization's endowment funds,"[36] it does not always happen that way.

As a matter of fact, in the book *Getting Started in Charitable Gift Giving: Your Guide to Planned Giving*, by Brian M. Sagrestano and Robert E. Wahlers, the assumption is that the realized planned gift will go into the endowment. There is even an equation: Planned Gifts = Endowment = Mission.[37] But as already noted, this calculation is not always accurate at least as far as the permanent endowment is concerned. Moreover, these authors suggest to gift planning professionals, "bequests designated for your general purposes give your organization the most flexibility to meet its needs when the bequest is realized. The best solution is flexible language that allows your organization to repurpose restricted bequests if your organization can no longer use the gift as the donor intended."[38] So, on the one hand, Sagrestano and Wahlers seem to support the concept that realized planned gifts, by definition, should be deposited into an endowment. They state that "the true measure of success for the case [for 'gift planning'] is how effectively the organization engages donors in the long-term mission and their desire to support your organization not for just today, but in perpetuity," and they also claim that the case "provides the rationale behind the request for legacy and endowment gifts."[39] On the other hand, it is unclear whether they mean the permanent endowment or that described by Mazur—restricted just in purpose but not for the permanent endowment—given the language just quoted. Also, by separating the words "legacy and endowment gifts," it is unclear whether these are considered the same or different entities.

In most of those organizations where I have consulted on endowment development, we have included language that clearly states that the gift "will be placed in [the organization's] Endowment Fund," although accounting practices in relation to that fund often differed. There was always a paragraph in marketing brochures describing how these monies would be managed and spent. However, there was one exception.

I was hired to help a small religious institution create an endowment program. One of our first conversations centered on the lack of and the necessity for an organizational by-law instructing how outright and future realized endowment gifts would be managed, invested, and spent. While the stated purpose of the effort was to build a permanent endowment and donors were solicited for that unambiguous goal, I could not persuade the group with which I worked to recommend to the board a specific by-law about how the resulting fund would operate. Each time we discussed the need to create such a policy, these individuals balked. They were very content with their current practice where the board decided what to do with gifts—whether outright donations intended for the endowment or those received sometime in the future.

After much cajoling on my part, this group finally came up with the following resolution: "The disposition of such gifts would be the responsibility of the Board. Recommended guidelines would be 75% of any contribution would be placed in the endowment and 25% used for immediate needs. In the case of an emergency, a majority of the board would have to approve current use of a gift." I always wondered what they would do with contributions that were directed by the donor to be deposited into the endowment.

While the board and this committee marketed its effort as building an endowment, there was no assurance that that would in effect be the end result. The group would not allow this resolution as to the disposition of realized gifts to be included in its promotional materials. The problem with being a consultant is that you can "push just so far." Moreover, for an organization, change is difficult.

There are options as to how organizations treat future gifts that are not directed by a donor to the permanent endowment. Some agree with Steven Meyers that the money should be used as needed when received or put into some kind of board-designated endowment fund. Greg Lassonde allows the $100,000 leeway in his proposed generic by-law, giving an organization some "wiggle room." Neal Myerberg, currently a planned giving consultant, lecturer in planned giving at Columbia University, and former chief executive officer for planned giving and endowments at UJA-Federation of New York, stated that when he advises or consults with an organization on endowment building, his policy is as follows: "I urge and teach organizations to place realized planned gifts above a certain size into some kind of a perpetual or term endowment. Often, it will be a board designated endowment fund, enabling the organization to use income pursuant to its spending rate for programs and purposes then in need of support. I emphasize that the realization of the gift is a one-time event and advise the board to look to the future by preserving these gifts wisely."[40]

In sum, Myerberg states the conundrum well. "Where an organization ultimately places realized legacies and unrestricted planned gifts is a challenge," he claims. "If the organization can support its operations from current revenues and strives to build a surplus of funds, it can set aside these monies for use in the future either in a perpetual endowment fund that allocates income only or in a quasi-endowment with discretion to use principal." He agrees that building an endowment is a "significant goal of planned giving" but acknowledges that all too many "organizations are unable or unwilling to be disciplined enough to keep legacy gifts for the future."[41]

PLANNED GIVING IS ONLY A TOOL

There is an understanding on the part of some in the fundraising field that a planned gift is by default an endowment contribution, and as I have explained, that was my assumption, too. But somehow the goal—the endowment—gets lost in the part—the mechanism for making it. As discussed above, while some organizations place realized deferred gifts in an endowment fund of some kind, it is not always the case.

An example of this contradiction becomes clear when on the one hand an organization suggests to donors that their bequest language state that funds should be used for its "general purposes" while at the same time authors like Sagrestano and Wahlers in *Getting Started in Charitable Gift Planning: Your Guide to Planned Giving* assume that planned gifts, which include bequests, are ultimately an endowment contribution. In their book, planned giving is the subject and the endowment is the assumption or maybe even default. And yet an explanation of endowment building per se is not included in the book, and as I have explained above, they simultaneously recommend language including "general purposes" with no mention of the permanent endowment.

I contend that the language is the problem; it is unclear. Planned gifts in and of themselves are often referred to in a way that makes them equal to an endowment, but they are not. When the countless courses and books about "planned giving" are reviewed, the focus is on the tools and not the purpose. It appears that the former is the end in itself when in fact it just a mechanism. And yet included in the title of numerous publications are the words "planned giving" as in Deborah Ashton's *The Complete Guide to Planned Giving* or in Sagrestano and Wahlers's *Getting Started in Charitable Gift Planning: Your Guide to Planned Giving.* In these books, planned giving is the subject matter and not the endowment fund, the purpose of which, I contend, is to receive those "planned gift" contributions in order to carry out the organizational "mission" far into the future. The realization of the planned gift is assumed to be the ultimate goal.[42] This seems to me to be an inversion of purpose.

If we were to use a gardening metaphor, the result of hard work and lots of tools—plants, compost, seedlings, rakes, trowels, etc.—is a lavish and flourishing garden. In relation to the subject of this book, planned giving is just one of the tools that can be used to build the endowment. There are others such as a by-law proposed herein or an outright gift designated for the permanent endowment. And yet planned giving seems to get all the attention, and those words, in and of themselves, are not even clear. Many authors even differentiate between bequests and planned giving, and while they do include the former in a list of tools describing the latter, they often dedicate whole chapters to bequests and describe all the "other" mechanisms for creating planned gifts in a separate discussion.[43]

If it is true that planned giving is only a tool and not the ultimate goal, which is in fact an endowment contribution, then it probably does not deserve its own fundraising department or course. It is no different than any other gift-giving mechanism, for example, an online donation or current, outright endowment contribution. It is a mechanism by which some asset is transferred to a charity by a donor. It really is not anything terribly fancy, and the most intricate gifts are usually designed by professional estate-planning advisers and thus only a recognition and basic knowledge of their various facets is probably required for fundraisers. (See chapter 8: "How to Build an Endowment Program.")

A statement of vision—the building of the permanent endowment—is the first step in creating an endowment program; this must be communicated to all stakeholders. Second, a by-law or a policy that instructs the staff and board how to handle realized deferred contributions, especially unrestricted ones, in terms of depositing them into a quasi-endowment fund is the next step. Such a directive eliminates any discussion or even conflict as to how such gifts will be used when received. Finally, prospects and donors must be specifically told of the priority.

Since the only real gift to a permanent endowment is the one designated by the donor according to UPMIFA, two additional things need to happen. First, not-for-profit organizations must change the language on their websites and in their marketing materials and not only clearly state donor options but also explain why these alternatives are important and what their implications mean to the charity and to the donor. In addition, in relation to the quasi-endowment, once it has been well discussed, there needs to be a by-law that states when and how a board can use the money not designated by the donor for a permanent endowment. All of this should be made clear in the documents, websites, and marketing materials so that a donor really knows what his or her choices are. In other words, I am recommending two steps for ensuring the growth of the permanent endowment. The first is a discussion by a board of what its goals are over time especially in relation to building for the long term, and then the second is describing the choices in language understandable to the donor so that he or she can make an educated decision in relation to a future gift.

This recommendation is clearly not limited to a new program—to the contrary. Doug White states that even the boards of programs that have been in existence for a long time need to review their procedures. He writes, "Generally . . . a planned gift is almost always marketed as a way to leave a legacy, which, if the money is spent right off doesn't actually happen; so the broader intent is not satisfied, even if the donor is unaware of the construct of the matter. And yes, specifically, in the sense that organizations need to give the process a lot more granular thought to this than most do. If they did, I imagine they would modify their by-laws in the way you describe." He continues, "As you say," given current behavior in so many not-for-profit organizations, "they threaten their future health."[44]

It is only with a clear statement of the importance of the permanent endowment and a by-law or policy that quasi-endowment funds will be managed and even spent according to the same procedures as the permanent fund, with exceptions that are clearly stated, that some change may happen in not-for-profit organizations. And it is only with understandable communication and transparency to donors that the permanent endowment will become a priority for them. Notwithstanding that so many leaders of not-for-profit organizations, both board and staff, claim that they need an endowment—particularly a permanent one—to ensure the future of their respective charities, only when they take these steps will this in fact happen. This recommendation is especially important since so many donors, I have been told, "trust" the organizations to which they leave gifts to use their contributions in ways that are "best for the institution." In my opinion, that is endowment building, especially the permanent kind.

CRASHING THE MATRIX

Steven L. Meyers is one of the few authors whom I have encountered who understands the need to change the language beyond charitable gift planning, legacy giving, and other such terms. While he, too, claims that "planned giving" as a subject has become obsolete, he agrees that it nevertheless lives on. He, like me, separates the tool from the goal but in the unique concept of "blended giving," which I think makes sense because it combines the endowment gift and the annual gift and uses meaningful language to do so.

Steven also believes that it is necessary to have "policies in place" although he focuses on how to *count* gifts while I focus on the *disposition* of the contribution. His wording is terrific: a "flexible endowment," which is often built from a combined future and current gift.[45] Steven is asking that we think outside of the traditional "planned, major, annual or capital" gift-giving classifications, and he doesn't even include the concept of endowment in this list because he, too, sees it as the end, not the process. He also remarks on the fact that trainers, whether consultants or instructors, "focus on tactics aimed squarely on advancing one type of gift."[46]

A lot of creativity is involved in Steven's idea of multi-faceted gift giving where endowment and annual contributions each have a role often in a complementary fashion. He refers to them as "building blocks" as opposed to "sequential, fragmented asks."[47] Steven understands and argues that often the terminology of fundraising—"annual, major, and planned gifts"—not only "mean nothing to donors and to their advisors," but such words could even serve as an "obstacle" to contributing. His is not a discussion of planned giving as an end-all; rather the focus is on the donor and his, her, or their ongoing contributions to multiple repositories, one of which is the permanent endowment. He separates the tool from the goal. He argues that this is still a challenge that is rarely addressed and not even considered in so many fund-development departments.[48]

I have found examples where blended gifts are not only encouraged but described in the marketing materials of an organization. For example, in the brochure entitled "Leading Together," published by St. Jude Children's Research Hospital, a couple who has made such a donation is featured and the title of their story is "A blended gift brings joy today and hope for tomorrow." An explanation of the contribution is included: "A blended gift generally refers to a charitable contribution that is comprised of a combination of an outright, immediate gift, along with a commitment to make a future gift through a will, trust or other revocable or irrevocable legacy gift." The brochure then describes the tools that these particular donors used: "an annual qualified charitable distribution from their IRA during their lifetime, and a separate donation to fund a St. Jude charitable gift annuity which will provide them with annual fixed payments—the remainder of which [after the death of the annuitants or recipients of the income stream] will go to St. Jude. The result will be a seven-figure gift that will help advance pediatric cancer research."[49]

In an interview with Steven Meyers, I asked him if a donor who established a blended gift while alive with an upfront payment and bequest promise had ever passed away and not provided the latter. He replied that it "probably" happened "but is pretty rare." He continued, "Our donors are deeply engaged with the organization [Weizmann Institute of Science]." Their gifts are "legally bookable commitments and [they] are locked in at various levels." They could make an "irrevocable commitment to a bequest through a pledge. They could provide a current sum of money for a specific number of years with the total commitment payable on death."[50]

I recently received a letter from the Office of Gift Planning of one of my alma maters. The letter was signed by the "bequest chairs," but gifts through a will or trust were not mentioned until the seventh paragraph, after, in the following order, a retirement account designation, charitable remainder trust, outright gift of a Required Minimum Distribution (RMD) from an IRA, and then charitable gift annuity. The words "estate gift" were used—another less than clear phrase—to encompass all of these gift-giving techniques. In addition, there was no mention as to how any of these donations would be used by the university when they were ultimately received. When I called the contact identified in the letter to ask, I was told that the contribution "is treated like an endowment in that only the income is used to support the activities of the school which does retain the right to use income and principal, if necessary, in any given year." In other words, from the school's perspective, there is a policy as to how any "estate gift" will ultimately be spent and that is in accordance with the needs of the school when the gift is realized. There was no mention of the permanent endowment in either the letter or discussion with the representative from the gift planning office.

Transparency in the disposition of realized bequests and other planned gifts is not consistent in the not-for-profit sector. The very clear formula introduced by Sagrestano and Wahlers—Planned Gifts = Endowment = Mission—is not always true especially in relation to the kind of endowment that is ultimately established by the recipient organization, if one is created at all. Even the use of the word "endowment" is not clear, and it depends upon the organization in question. While a planned gift may be intended to meet the mission of the organization, it does not always end up in the endowment or at least one that is "permanent" or "true." Therefore, those organizations with the specific goal of building such a fund must begin by creating policies about how future, unrestricted donations will be used, and these must be translated into a language that donors can clearly understand. They will then know how a planned gift, future gift, legacy gift, personalized gift, donor-centered gift, and so forth will be spent when it is ultimately received. Organizations need to explain their preferences as well as implications for gift giving to donors and not only to those who call a fundraising office for information but those who do not and rely on other sources of information whether they be print marketing materials or a website.

NOTES

1. I think one of the best series of articles describing this Act is by Frank A. Monti and appears in *Inside Philanthropy* as a column entitled "The Gift Advisor." See "A Close Look at the Law Governing Endowment Funds," March 10, 2015.
2. Monti, "A Close Look."
3. Douglas White, e-mail to author, March 18, 2020.
4. David J. Chused, e-mail to author, April 24, 2020.
5. David J. Chused wrote the following to the author in an e-mail dated Monday, May 11, 2010: "Words to this same or similar affect will also result in a true endowed fund. For example, 'I direct that only the earnings from my gift are used to support [the stated purpose]' or 'It is my wish that gift principal not be used in furtherance of [the stated purpose].'"
6. Columbia University website, https://finance.columbia.edu/frequently-asked-questions/358.
7. United States Holocaust Memorial Museum, "The Planned Giving Newsletter," Fall 2014.
8. Linda Mazur, e-mail to author, April 28, 2020.
9. The Episcopal Church Foundation website, https://www.episcopalfoundation.org/programs/endowment-management-solutions/restricted-vs-unrestricted.
10. The Episcopal Church Foundation website.
11. The Episcopal Church Foundation website.
12. East Texas Communities Foundation, "Policy For Nonprofit Endowment Funds," 2011, https://etcf.org/wp-content/uploads/2016/11/PolicyForNonprofitEndowmentFunds05202011-1.pdf.
13. The San Diego Foundation website, https://www.sdfoundation.org/news-events/sdf-news/endowment-funds-vs-nonendowment-funds-whats-difference.
14. The San Diego Foundation website. In my work with Jewish community foundations, our ultimate goal was always to build the unrestricted endowment. Therefore, we created minimum gift policies relating to donor-advised funds (DAF). We required a sum of $10,000 to establish a DAF, and if a balance fell below that amount, the donor was given six months to bring the balance in the fund to that level. If that did not happen, the remaining monies in the fund were swept into the permanent endowment. If contributors chose to move their entire fund to some other not-for-profit entity, we kept $10,000 of the total in the DAF, transferred it to the unrestricted endowment, and maintained the name of the fund assigned by the donor.
15. Henry & Horne, "Top 12 Points to Avoid Endowment Confusion," *The 501S(cene)*, February 19, 2013, https://www.hhcpa.com/blogs/non-profit-accounting-services/top-12-points-to-avoid-endowment-confusion.
16. Hurwit and Associates, "Confusing Gift Terms, 2017," https://www.hurwitassociates.com/major-gifts-grants-restricted-funds/confusing-gift-terms?A=SearchResult&SearchID=12298918&ObjectID=4722747&ObjectType=35.
17. Ellis Carter, "Permanent Endowment = Infinity and Beyond," *Charity Lawyer: Nonprofit Law Simplified*, September 23, 2009.
18. The Fund Raising School, Lilly Family School of Philanthropy, Indiana University, Indianapolis, "Planned Giving: Getting the Proper Start," 17.
19. The Fund Raising School, "Planned Giving," 15.
20. The Fund Raising School, "Planned Giving," 17.
21. The Fund Raising School, "Planned Giving," 136.
22. The Fund Raising School, "Planned Giving," 311.

23. Adrian Sargeant, Jen Shang, and associates, *Fundraising Principles and Practice*, 2nd ed. (Hoboken, NJ: John Wiley & Sons, 2017), 501.

24. Sargeant and Shang, *Fundraising Principles and Practice*, 516.

25. Sargeant and Shang, *Fundraising Principles and Practice*, 524.

26. Sargeant and Shang, *Fundraising Principles and Practice*, 501.

27. Monti, "A Close Look."

28. Monti, "A Close Look."

29. Steven Meyers, e-mail to author, February 3, 2020

30. Steven Meyers, e-mail to author, February 3, 2020.

31. Scott C. Stevenson, "How to Start an Endowment for Your Nonprofit," September 16, 2019, https://www.thebalancesmb.com/how-to-start-an-endowment-for-your-nonprofit-2502103.

32. Bylaws of Combined Jewish Philanthropies of Greater Boston, Inc. as amended and restated May 16, 2019. Interestingly, the Jewish Federation of South Palm Beach County, Inc. maintains a similar resolution but states that "all non-specific bequests or gifts received by the Federation, in the amount of twenty-five thousand dollars ($25,000) or less will be credited to the Federation unrestricted annual campaign in the fiscal year received" (Jewish Federation of South Palm Beach County, Inc., Executive Committee Meeting 30 October 2014, Board of Directors Meeting 30 October 2014, Resolution to Revise Foundation's Unrestricted Funds Annual Spending Policies 2015–16 Fiscal Year). In other words, while the Combined Jewish Philanthropies uses $1,000 and the South Palm Beach Philanthropies $25,000, the point of these examples is to demonstrate that the institutions have the right to make their own guidelines and that the endowment is the default repository notwithstanding the differing gift amounts.

33. Charles Glassenberg, e-mail to author, April 27, 2020.

34. Greg Lassonde, e-mail to author, May 11, 2020.

35. Greg Lassonde, e-mail to author, December 30, 2019.

36. Stanley Weinstein and Pamela Barden, *The Complete Guide to Fundraising Management*, 4th ed. (Hoboken, NJ: John Wiley and Sons, 2017), 204.

37. Brian Sagrestano and Robert E. Wahlers, *Getting Started in Charitable Gift Planning: Your Guide to Planned Giving* (Nashville: CharityChannel Press, 2016), 17.

38. Sagrestano and Wahlers, *Getting Started in Charitable Gift Planning*, 9.

39. Sagrestano and Wahlers, *Getting Started in Charitable Gift Planning*, 54–55.

40. Neal Myerberg, telephone interview with author, December 12, 2019, and subsequent e-mail, May 4, 2020.

41. Neal Myerberg, telephone interview, December 12, 2019, and subsequent e-mail.

42. Sagrestano and Wahlers, *Getting Started in Charitable Gift Planning*.

43. See, for example, Sargeant and Shang, *Fundraising Principles and Practice*.

44. Douglas White, e-mail to author, March 18, 2020.

45. Steven L. Meyers, *Personalized Philanthropy: Crash the Fundraising Matrix* (Nashville: CharityChannel Press, 2015), 11.

46. Meyers, *Personalized Philanthropy*, 20.

47. Meyers, *Personalized Philanthropy*, 14.

48. Meyers, *Personalized Philanthropy*, xxii.

49. St. Jude Children's Research Hospital, "Leading Together," 10.

50. Steven Meyers, conversation with author, December 9, 2019.

Chapter Three

Why We Need an Endowment—or Maybe We Don't

There are many conflicting opinions as to whether not-for-profit organizations should even be building permanent endowment funds. There are those who think it is important to do so in order to ensure that an organization is able to deliver services in the future at the same rate as it does today—in other words, at the very minimum to keep up with inflation. This argument primarily states that in order to maintain "intergenerational equity" where the "claims of the present" do not supersede those still to come, an endowment is maintained and invested to guarantee future and equal spending power. According to Nobel prize–winning economist James Tobin, "The trustees of an endowed institution are the guardians of the future against the claims of the present. Their task is to preserve equity among generations."[1]

Another and not inconsistent rationale for maintaining and building an endowment is to provide stability to operations especially when times are tough whether due to issues in the economy or a change in donor support by individuals, a foundation, or the government. An endowment fund "act[s] as an insurance policy for the future. With an endowment, facing the ups and downs of the economy and fundraising becomes easier," writes Scott Stevenson, author of articles and books on not-for-profit organizations. He continues, "An endowment helps diversify your organization's income and reduces your vulnerability to every economic crisis."[2]

Some authors claim that endowment building is good for particular organizations such as museums but not necessarily for all not-for-profits.[3] This seems to me to "go without saying" since so many organizations can barely get by on their current budgets and/or their missions, hopefully, may not even exist in the future (e.g., peace building in the Middle East or the eradication of breast cancer). Some organizations are just too new and have not had time to foster one of the necessary requirements for endowment gifts—donor loyalty.

There are those arguments that come down somewhere in the middle. Maybe there is an alternative to endowment building such as an "aspirational impact fund," which, according to consultant Alan Cantor, is a "hybrid" that is designed to last a certain amount of time wherein "both principal and interest would be spent down over the course of 10 years. The money would be invested conservatively, given the time horizon."[4]

A new study by the Rockefeller Philanthropy Advisors and Campden Wealth entitled "Global Trends and Strategic Time Horizons in Family Philanthropy 2020" found that "more donors are proactively considering the time horizon of their philanthropy, weighing whether it is more effective to have a pre-determined end date for philanthropic initiatives or to continue in perpetuity."[5] The findings are "based on a survey of 201 families of significant wealth who are engaged in philanthropic giving," and the report states that "as donors become more sophisticated in giving and investing, they're thinking seriously about the time horizon that makes the most sense for the goals, motivations and visions of their own philanthropy."[6]

The report claims that one of the most immediate concerns of donors is "impact," notwithstanding what time horizon they choose—short or long. But for the ones with a "time-limited approach to their philanthropy," they want to "see the impact of giving during their lifetime." They have a "narrow philanthropic focus," and they are interested in transferring "more of a founding donor's wealth to good causes sooner than later." However, notwithstanding a trend toward this time-limited approach and "concentrating donations over shorter time periods," the report concludes that "the majority of responding families (62%) have adopted the more traditional in-perpetuity model of philanthropy."[7] A University of Chicago study noted that an even larger percentage are assuming the "old fashioned model": 71 percent of foundations are "created in perpetuity."[8]

There are two sets of "drivers" that influence the time horizons adopted by family foundations, according to a *New York Times* article entitled "Trading the Perpetual Drip for a Philanthropic Flood."[9] For those that choose to spend down their respective endowments, the primary focus is, as described above, having an immediate impact that "can be seen and assessed."[10] On the other hand, those that maintain a "traditional" focus are "motivated to address continuing problems, strengthen their family values and purpose, and have an impact on beneficiaries over several generations."[11] These are very different perspectives, and while the nature and tax structure of the organizations are dissimilar—a family foundation versus an institutional-based endowment—the question and dilemma of endowment maintenance over time for the benefit of multiple generations versus short-term spending and immediately realized impact are similar. In the case of both kinds of foundations described in the Rockefeller Philanthropy Advisors report as well as *The New York Times* article—spend down and the "traditional" ones—some of the key words that appear repeatedly are also ubiquitous in the area of endowment building—"impact," "time-horizon," "rate of spending," and "generations." "Values" is another word that is regularly used.

Interestingly, the Andrea and Charles Bronfman Foundation chose the spend down route while simultaneously creating what Jeffrey Solomon, former chief executive officer of the foundation, calls "virtual endowments," a concept described in chapter 2 as a blended gift. He wrote, "We have utilized 'virtual endowments' with any number of long term supported organizations. In these, we make a lifetime annual gift of 5% of the bequest in Charles' [Bronfman] estate plan for their endowments."[12] In this case the Bronfman Foundation balanced the concepts of sunsetting with ongoing support of select organizations. Solomon explained that the criteria for the latter were "a very sustainable organization" that had the ability "to manage an endowment. We were very careful about what kinds of organizations we chose for [virtual endowments]." They were institutions that had a "track record" with "managed endowments."[13] With some organizations, however, the foundation makes distributions "to a third party (e.g. community foundation), which only distributes the income from the endowment to the recipient organization."[14] It seems that the Bronfman Foundation in fact took two routes: it established quasi-endowments where, with a vote of a board, a recipient organization can decide to use principal; but where there was less confidence in a charity's financial management, the permanent endowment was chosen, using another organization as the vehicle to manage and allocate funds according to a spending policy. No use of principal is allowed in this second choice.

My first introduction to these various perspectives about endowment building came many years ago before I even began working in the field of fundraising in general and endowment development in particular. I was a research associate at Yale University's Program on Non-Profit Organizations, where I became intrigued by the work of Henry Hansmann, who was a scholar at the Yale Law School and who wrote about the rationale or lack thereof for maintaining endowments.[15] While most of his work related to university-based funds, especially at large institutions such as Harvard and Yale, he questioned the justification for holding so much money in abeyance when it could have been used to support students who needed current help in order to pay tuition or for essentials of daily life on campus. Hansmann argued that future generations are more likely to be wealthier than present ones given historical patterns, and therefore, putting money away "deprives the relatively poor to subsidize the relatively rich." He writes in favor of adopting a "purposive" approach to using endowments, which could include "occasions when saving large sums for the future is appropriate" but where current spending is also considered as part of "rational long-range financial planning." He recommends using "discretionary reserves as a financial buffer, with all the flexibility, and all the difficulty of judgement, that doing so implies."[16] In other words, he prefers the quasi-endowment to the permanent, notwithstanding that he understands the need for the latter, too.

Agreeing for the most part with Hansmann that monies should not be put away into an endowment in perpetuity, Charlene Seidle argues her case in far stronger language than he. She claims that "endowments consume capital that, from a policy perspective, should be available for experimentation and aggressive risk-taking, and in doing so they actually prevent problem-solving."[17] Seidle writes that "every dollar we put into endowment for a specific organization or prescribed cause robs both the current generation AND the future generation." She explains that it robs "the current generation because these are funds not being invested in solving current social problems. Instead, we perpetuate a bad system by passing on the problems we have created." She claims that current decision-makers are in fact "arrogant." They are telling "the future generation . . . that we have no confidence in their ability to decide which organizations will thrive and which should be shut down. We are communicating that complacency is valued and that an organization that has long outlived its core mission of effectiveness should still be in business simply because WE think it is important now."[18]

Seidle argues against the position taken by James Tobin as described in the first paragraph of this chapter. She writes, "A focus on current endowment building in particular perpetuates intergenerational inequities as we kick the can down the road. Solving the problem or at least taking the most risk in aggressively doing so is the best equity we can create for future generations."[19]

Seidle claims in the title of her piece that it is "Time to Sunset Perpetuity."[20] I blanched when I read those words because in all of the work that I did in raising endowment funds, I frequently used the expression "in perpetuity" to describe the purpose of the effort. For example, when I worked for Jewish federations, we referred to funds that were established to support the annual campaign after the death of the donor as "Named Perpetual Annual Campaign Endowment Funds." We used the word "perpetuity" to describe the purpose of the endowment contribution: "Ultimately, the donor will have the satisfaction of knowing that he or she has made a gift that will benefit the [name of organization] in perpetuity."[21] And we explained that in relation to a gift of life insurance, it is "traditionally" a "gift of love for your family, but it can also be used to perpetuate something you cherish, something whose future you would like to help guarantee."[22]

And I did not limit these words to my work in the Jewish community. In a booklet to describe a new endowment initiative for a theater, I wrote, "Through a legacy contribution—either lifetime or by bequest—your gift will remain in perpetuity."[23] That word appears regularly in so many of the materials that I drafted for innumerable clients in various areas of service, including senior housing, public broadcasting, and education.

Even in my first book, *Donor Cultivation and the Donor Lifecycle Map: A New Framework for Fundraising*, when explaining how a potential endowment gift might be described to a donor, I wrote, "It is better referred to in terms of how the contribution will be remembered or what impact the [donor] might have that lasts for a lifetime and beyond or what we sometimes call 'in perpetuity'—however long that may be."[24] Alan Cantor reminds us "that perpetuity is a very, very long time indeed."[25]

There are writers who favor endowment building for any number of reasons. For example, Dennis R. Hammond, in an article entitled "Endowments Are Not a Luxury," claims that endowment development allows good financial management as well as intergenerational support. He states that "the rationale is simple: Save today, spend tomorrow." He continues, "Preservation and growth of seed capital have long been basic tenets of financial strategy, and especially so for nonprofit institutions whose annual expenses are not consistently matched by revenues."[26] He disagrees with the position of Hansmann and Seidle: "It is tempting to put today's needs ahead of tomorrow's, especially when current decision makers won't be around to ascertain the outcome or be held accountable for it. Nevertheless, the concept of intergenerational equity cannot be abandoned." He writes, "An endowment, properly managed, will support the same programs 50 years from now, net after inflation, that it supports today. The income from new additions to the endowment may be used to finance new programs, offer additional scholarships, or simply provide a deeper bulwark against the distant unknown."[27]

This is clearly the message communicated by the United States Holocaust Memorial Museum in materials describing the purpose of its endowment: "to secure the Museum's global impact in an uncertain future."[28] "Uncertainty" is the key word, and for Seidle it is too, but she is arguing that because of that "uncertainty," we should focus on addressing issues today and not build endowment funds for the future.[29]

Alan Cantor claims that endowment funds are good for museums because "at their core, they exist to preserve valuable art and artifacts. Building an endowment at a museum helps guarantee the organization's infrastructure so that it can meet its mission in perpetuity."[30] This is also the theme of a 2012 article in *The New York Times*, "How an Acquisition Fund Burnishes Reputations."[31] So, I guess for museums, the building of endowments is acceptable particularly when it comes to purchases for collections.

However, endowment development is certainly not limited to museums or any other kind of not-for-profit organization. Moreover, it has many benefits albeit for institutions that have the capacity to raise these monies and the long-term mission that will benefit from them. There is no doubt that reliable income from a permanent endowment relieves pressure on budgets notwith-standing that there may be some additional costs in relation to creating and maintaining it. In the long run, these are balanced by the financial benefits. I am not an economist and so I do not look at the issue in terms of intergenera-tional parity, but I do understand endowment building from two points of view—one is that of the organization and its board of trustees trying to manage a budget, and the other is from that of the donor who wants to make an impact on an institution and leave a legacy but may not have current resources to do so or a sufficient amount given the minimum requirements that some not-for-profit organizations mandate for a named, permanent fund.

Another argument for building an endowment is to even out spending over time and/or provide monies when economic periods are difficult and annual fundraising cannot meet the budgetary demands of an organization. Many of the writers cited above focus on using monies to address current needs or to achieve present-day impact, but they do not mention what hap-pens when there are shortfalls in available funds because of a recession or other stress factors. Maybe a donor, who provided a large annual gift, decides to change focus and cuts a contribution in its entirety. (Usually, in these cases, the donor gives the organization some notice, but sometimes not.) Or maybe this same contributor has a fall-out with a member of the agency's staff or disagrees with a policy position and simply stops giving. I have seen that happen so many times in my career. On occasion a donor has a bad financial year and cannot maintain his or her traditional support. And what about those organizations who depend upon government grants for certain programs and these become "squeezed" or cut entirely?[32] How will the ser-vices and salaries that these monies once supported be provided? A perma-nent endowment secures a flow of income into the annual budget that in difficult times maintains an organization's ability to continue operating.

There is also the issue related to the quasi or board-directed endowment fund. If that fund can be used over time notwithstanding spending restric-tions, or as Steven Meyers describes with "inconvenience" or as Jeffrey Solomon states with a built-in requirement that a "super majority of board members" must approve an allocation, then these savings can ultimately be dissipated and the "cushion" and flexibility that they are supposed to provide cease to exist.

Hammond summarizes the issue well. He explains, "There will be inevi-table periods of conflict between short-term operational needs and the long-term need for growth and maintenance." He says that board members will have to "evaluate their institutions' idiosyncratic needs during market or operational shocks." He disagrees with Hansmann's contention "that future generations of patrons, students, and donors will have more money tomorrow than they do today," and as a result they will support charitable organizations in their own time. He states that "unfortunately, [that] argument is to prudence as gambling is to saving." He concludes, "In that ambiguous art of balancing present and future demands, one fact remains unambiguous: Endowments are not a luxury but a necessity."[33]

I first recognized this issue in 1987 when I was hired to start a new endowment program for the Jewish Federation in Springfield, Massachusetts. The stock market famously dropped that fall—approximately 25 percent in a few days. Everyone in the federation was alarmed since we recognized that our donors and probably those of every other charity would most likely reduce their traditional commitments as a result.

At the time the federation had a very small permanent endowment. On the other hand, several individuals had established donor-advised funds (DAF) that were managed along with the endowment, and if it were not for those contributions, we would not have been able to meet ours nor any of our agencies' needs. (The Jewish Federation operates somewhat like a United Way—as an umbrella organization that allocates centrally raised funds to member and sometimes non-member agencies or service providers.)

I was negative about DAFs at the time. I felt that these were established primarily for their tax advantages as well as the charitable preferences of the contributors. I did not view them as benefiting the community as a whole. This was because the donors retained the right to "recommend" distributions from these donor-advised funds, and notwithstanding that they were managed as part of our endowment, they could be spent down at any time. (This latter rule has been changed in most Jewish federation foundations and a "floor" is required for the majority of DAFs.) My preference, even then, was for unrestricted, permanent endowment monies that would be available in emergencies as well as for other purposes, such as research and demonstration projects for which there was never much financial support. However, if it were not for distributions from these donor-advised funds, the federation would have faced stark circumstances where many people—old, young, immigrant, and poor—would have been without help. While these DAF monies were not permanent endowment funds, they had been put away in a so-called bank account and were available when needed. The point is that had the money not been saved by donors during good times, it would not have been available during the market downturn. At the same time, many of us in the not-for-profit sector have come to realize that it cannot depend on distributions from donor-advised funds, notwithstanding how popular they have become, to provide future safety nets. We need a permanent endowment.

This is also Dennis Hammond's argument: "Prudence demands, and common law encourages, institutions to set aside some of each year's earnings, together with gifts given in perpetuity, to help maintain operations in future years when revenues, earnings, and gifts to the annual fund are inadequate."[34]

Notwithstanding that endowment monies can provide support to annual budgets as well as address emergencies when they occur, I like another purpose—to provide funds for studies and demonstration projects in the not-for-profit sector. These are difficult to launch and maintain through the regular budgetary process of most charitable organizations. I always explained to prospective endowment donors that unlike in the for-profit sector, most non-profit organizations do not have available funds to try new approaches except if they are institutions with dedicated research departments such as universities. In most community organizations, research is a luxury, and yet there is a constant pursuit to improve how services are delivered and to find new ways to approach problems. An article in *The Chronicle of Philanthropy* supports this position. The writers state that "even if an organization never suffers an economic blow that drives it to dig into its reserves, that cash on hand might provide the small margin for innovation and discovery that is the only means a grant-driven organization has to develop new projects."[35] I maintain that this statement is true for most not-for-profit organizations, not just "grant-driven" ones. Distributions from endowment funds provide resources for taking risks—what Seidle advocates, however in the short term as opposed to over time.

FROM THE PERSPECTIVE OF THE DONOR

There are donors who cannot make substantive gifts from current assets but who want to support charities in a way that is meaningful to them and hopefully to the recipient organization, too. These are the people who Simone P. Joyaux calls "loyal donors" notwithstanding that they might not be "major" in today's parlance, which she dismisses as truly unfair to those whose gift might be "more special and important" to them than the contributions of the incredibly wealthy whose support might carry much less personal meaning. She claims that these individuals with modest assets might contribute "the largest gift" they ever make through their estate,[36] and these are the donors whom we must include in all of our fundraising strategic plans. We also have the responsibility to ensure that their ultimate gifts retain significance in terms of the way in which we honor and remember them.

Endowment fundraising has an extraordinary opportunity to celebrate the contributions of all donors no matter the size of their respective donations, and that is a purpose that I endorse. If done correctly, this type of development is not about "bringing in the greenbacks" that one interviewee told me was the common denominator of most fundraising departments. It is about creating legacies and purpose for a contributor. This is why I think it is important that donors understand their choices in terms of making these gifts and that organizations have an obligation to be clear as to how they will be used depending on the form that the contributor selects. From the perspective of the donor, an endowment gift can provide a meaningful and lasting legacy that is illustrative or reflective of what was important to him or her during his or her lifetime. This is a mighty purpose.

And as a postscript, an interesting article in *The New York Times* convinced me of the value of the permanent endowment. The article was about a woman, "Paula Volent, the head of the Bowdoin College endowment." It really had nothing to do with the concept of endowment building and everything to do with describing "one of the nation's most successful endowment managers." But a quote by her confirmed for me the value of endowment development. She stated, "Aside from its financial rewards, managing a college endowment is a way of doing good. A rising endowment can give 'students who could not otherwise afford to get an education the chance to get one.'" And the article reports, "In the 2018 fiscal year . . . the endowment provided roughly three-quarters of the school's $41.6 million financial aid budget."[37] That is powerful.

NOTES

1. Quoted in Sorrel R. Paskin, "How Much Endowment Is Enough," National Association of Independent Schools, February 21, 2012.

2. Scott C. Stevenson, "How to Start an Endowment for Your Nonprofit," https://www.thebalancesmb.com/how-to-start-an-endowment-for-your-nonprofit-2502103.

3. Judith H. Dobrzynski, "How an Acquisition Fund Burnishes Reputations," *The New York Times*, March 15, 2012, p. F-4.

4. Alan Cantor, "An Approach to Funding That Might Actually Work," Alan Cantor Consulting Blog, March 16, 2012, https://alancantorconsulting.wordpress.com/2012/03/16/an-approach-to-funding-that-might-actually-work/.

5. Rockefeller Philanthropy Advisors, "Future Trends for Strategic Philanthropy: Survey Reveals More Wealthy Families Want to Donate During Their Lifetimes: Education Remains Most Popular Cause," January 21, 2020, https://www.rockpa.org/future-trends-for-strategic-philanthropy-survey-reveals-more-wealthy-families-want-to-donate-during-their-lifetimes-education-remains-most-popular-cause/.

6. Rockefeller Philanthropy Advisors, "Future Trends for Strategic Philanthropy."

7. Rockefeller Philanthropy Advisors, "Future Trends for Strategic Philanthropy."

8. Paul Sullivan, "Wealth Matters: Trading the Perpetual Drip for a Philanthropic Flood," *The New York Times*, January 18, 2020, B7.

9. Rockefeller Philanthropy Advisors, "Future Trends for Strategic Philanthropy."

10. Rockefeller Philanthropy Advisors, "Future Trends for Strategic Philanthropy."

11. Sullivan, "Wealth Matters."

12. Jeffrey R. Solomon, telephone conversation with author, January 18, 2020.

13. Jeffrey R. Solomon, e-mail to author, February 17, 2020.

14. Jeffrey R. Solomon, e-mail to author, May 14, 2020.

15. Hansmann is currently the Oscar M. Ruebhausen Professor Emeritus of Law and Professorial Lecturer in Law at Yale Law School.

16. Henry Hansmann, "Bigger Is Not Necessarily Better, *The Chronicle of Philanthropy*, May 27–28, 2014.

17. Charlene Seidle, "Now's the Time to Sunset Perpetuity," eJewishPhilanthropy, January 11, 2016.

18. Seidle, "Now's the Time to Sunset Perpetuity."

19. Seidle, "Now's the Time to Sunset Perpetuity."
20. Seidle, "Now's the Time to Sunset Perpetuity."
21. Jewish Foundation of Greater New Haven, 1993.
22. Jewish Foundation of Greater New Haven, 1993.
23. Goodspeed Musicals, "Preserve the Legacy of Musical Theatre," 2002.
24. Deborah Kaplan Polivy, *Donor Cultivation and the Door Lifecycle Map: A New Framework for Fundraising* (Hoboken, NJ: John Wiley and Sons, 2014), 138.
25. Alan Cantor, "Endowments, Pro and Con," Alan Cantor Consulting Blog, November 7, 2012, https://www.alancantorconsulting.com/2012/11/endowments-pro-and-con/.
26. Dennis R. Hammond, "Endowments Are Not a Luxury," *The Chronicle of Philanthropy*, May 27–28, 2004.
27. Hammond's article is juxtaposed to Hansmann in a piece entitled, "Pro & Con: Are Endowments A Good Idea?"
28. The Planned Giving Newsletter of the United States Holocaust Memorial Museum, Summer 2013, page 1.
29. Seidle, "Now's the Time to Sunset Perpetuity."
30. Cantor, "Endowments, Pro and Con."
31. Dobrzynski, "How an Acquisition Fund Burnishes Reputations."
32. Hammond, "Endowments Are Not a Luxury."
33. Hammond, "Endowments Are Not a Luxury."
34. Hammond, "Endowments Are Not a Luxury."
35. Stephanie J. Hull and Phil Buchanan, "It's Time to End Nonprofits' Hand-to-Mouth Way of Life," *The Chronicle of Philanthropy*, April 28, 2020, https://www.philanthropy.com/article/It-s-Time-to-End/248646.
36. Simone Joyaux, "Fundraising Vocabulary: Words I Hate," CharityChannel Press, June 26, 2018, https://charitychannel.com/fundraising-vocabulary-words-i-hate/.
37. Geraldine Fabrikant, "A College Investor Who Beats the Ivys," *The New York Times*, March 24, 2019, BU1.

Chapter Four

A Case Study

*The Life & Legacy Program of the
Harold Grinspoon Foundation*

Endowment building is the clear goal of Life & Legacy, a national program of the Harold Grinspoon Foundation (HGF) located in Springfield, Massachusetts.[1] The website and all written material describing Life & Legacy state that its objective is to build "permanent endowments that will sustain vibrant Jewish communities for years to come."[2] The Grinspoon Foundation has invested in excess of $16.5 million dollars in this project since its inception in 2012,[3] and it estimates that this sum will have raised $1 billion in legacy commitments of which more than $100 million will have been placed in organizational endowments by the spring of 2020.[4] The purpose of including this case study is to highlight not only its singular goal of building permanent endowment funds but also to provide a model that could be replicated in whole or in part by other funders that recognize and support a similar endowment-building challenge within the not-for-profit sector.

Life & Legacy is built on the idea of encouraging individuals to sign a Letter of Intent to leave a legacy to the local Jewish community and in particular to one or more of its agencies or synagogues[5] and then to document that commitment in an actual gift whether it be future or current, income producing or not. But this is only the beginning.

There are additional elements that are integral to the program. The first is a partnership between the Grinspoon Foundation and a local Jewish federation or Jewish community foundation[6] that agrees to manage the project on a community-wide basis. The second component is the participation of community organizations or agencies (usually from ten to fifteen depending on the size of the respective population) to work cooperatively with the federation or foundation to obtain the Letters of Intent and documented commitments from their respective supporters. Third is a matching grant for funding of the program from the Harold Grinspoon Foundation to the federation or foundation. Fourth are incentive grants to the respective community agencies for reaching goals in relation to obtaining the Letters of Intent and documentation of actual gifts. The fifth component of the program, which is essential to its overall success, is the training and mentoring that the Grinspoon Foundation's staff provides to all the participating organizations. Together these ingredients make the Life & Legacy program stellar in its commitment to endowment building.

Essential Ingredients of LIFE & LEGACY

1. A partnership with a local Jewish federation or foundation that contracts to oversee the implementation of the program on a city-wide and/or regional basis.
2. Participation of community organizations that agree to join with the Jewish federation or foundation in the program.
3. Budget support to the federation/foundation by the Grinspoon Foundation.
4. Financial incentives to the local community organizations to motivate them to reach specific legacy commitment goals.
5. Ongoing mentoring and training from the Harold Grinspoon Foundation.
6. A signed Declaration of Intent followed by a formal commitment to leave a legacy gift to an organization(s) within a local community.

Life & Legacy works like this. Jewish federations or Jewish community foundations apply to the Harold Grinspoon Foundation for acceptance into the program, and once they are admitted, they sign a formal contract with the Foundation that specifies guidelines for involvement. For example, the federation or foundation must agree to hire a new or assign an existing staff person to manage the initiative at a minimum of three days per week. They must also enlist a minimum of ten community organizations to participate. The federation/foundation is required to pay two-thirds of the program's costs, which the Harold Grinspoon Foundation will match on a one-third basis up to $100,000 annually over the length of the project, which currently extends for four years. In other words, the Foundation will invest up to $400,000 in a community to encourage endowment building. This is a significant commitment.

The local participating organizations must also sign a contract in order to join the program, but in their case, it is with the federation/foundation as opposed to the Grinspoon Foundation. As part of their agreement, these institutions must form a Legacy Committee of between four and six people, one of whom must be a professional employee of the organization and the others are identified as "key lay leaders" or what is commonly referred to as volunteers. Their primary responsibility is to meet the goals that they have set for their own organization, such as hold a minimum number of conversations with supporters about Letters of Intent and attend Life & Legacy training sessions. In addition, all of these organizations agree to place any realized legacy commitments that result from the program into a permanent endowment fund. Some federations/foundations require that they manage this money while others allow these contributions to be invested by another licensed entity chosen by the organization. There are other requirements for joining Life & Legacy, but these are the essential ones.

Once all of these agreements are signed, the actual implementation of the program begins first with visits and training by the Grinspoon Foundation's national Life & Legacy staff followed by the writing of an organizational legacy plan, which, for the most part, includes the following components: a case statement developed by each participating institution describing the impact it has on the community; procedures for managing the program; identification of the specific roles of the team members; a list of prospects; proposed methods for promoting and publicizing the concept of legacy giving; and procedures for demonstrating appreciation and gratitude to those who sign the Letters of Intent and document their respective gifts as well as publicly recognizing these participants.[7]

Various methods are suggested to persuade individuals to sign the Letters and document their respective gifts. These include personal telephone calls, marketing materials, special events, announcements at functions, and more. The signing of the intent commitment and then formalization of the gift are each considered milestones that, when a specific number is achieved (the goals), are rewarded in the form of incentive grants. The Grinspoon Foundation offers minimum incentive grant awards of $5,000 per organization in the first two years of the program for achieving legacy commitment targets and recommends that the federation/foundation establish "tiered incentive grants so the local organizations keep moving once they have momentum rather than stopping when they reach the goal."[8] There are additional inducements for achieving legacy gift formalization objectives in the third and fourth years of the program. One of the unique features of Life & Legacy is that contributors can designate a gift to more than one organization and the federation/foundation facilitates that process.

Templates for the Letters of Intent and Legacy Gift Confirmations along with descriptions of gift options and model thank you notes are provided by the Grinspoon Foundation. There are also "Tip" sheets for all aspects of the program including suggestions for having a conversation with potential Letters of Intent signers, formalizing gifts, and sustaining an organization's legacy initiative once the official program concludes. The Life & Legacy website offers a multitude of resources that can be accessed by participating organizations.[9]

The Grinspoon Foundation occasionally provides its partner communities with small presents to be given to individuals who have signed a Letter of Intent as a way of expressing appreciation and gratitude for a donor's commitment. In 2019, for example, "as a one-time activity," thirteen thousand boxes of Hanukah candles including a "personalized belly band printed with 'Thank You for Lighting the Way' were distributed to communities that pre-ordered them." National Director Arlene D. Schiff explained that "our reasons for offering these gifts free of charge as our budget allows is to make it easier for organizations with limited resources to appropriately steward their donors." An objective of the program is to ensure organizations integrate effective donor support and encouragement into their organizational culture "so that they can continue to do so on their own for the long term."[10]

Success is measured first by the number of Letters of Intent secured and then by the percentage of these that become legalized commitments. The value of the latter is calculated using an average realized gift of $25,000, and this estimate is based on "national averages for legacy commitments," according to Schiff. She explained that the typical range of realized bequests is $32,000 to $72,000 and "so we decided to be very conservative and use $25,000 if a donor doesn't disclose the value of the gift or they let us know it's a percentage of some asset. A few of our larger communities use $50,000 as the average because that is their actual experience. The small federations use $10,000. We know [that] we are going to get gifts ranging from $1,000 to $1M." Only those contributions that are the result of a donor signing a Letter of Intent are included in the estimated future total.[11]

The goal of the program is not only to ensure that the participating organizations have a future flow of endowment monies but also to achieve a transformative change wherein "legacy giving is celebrated and it becomes a normative activity," explained Winnie Sandler Grinspoon, president of the Harold Grinspoon Foundation. She states that the program benefits an entire community "and not just a singular organization."[12] As a matter of fact, Life & Legacy has become such a well-known and integral part of Jewish communal fundraising that it was featured in *The Chronicle of Philanthropy*.[13]

The word "legacy" means "bequeathed by will"[14] according to the dictionary, and this bequest-making mechanism is one of the primary vehicles that Life & Legacy encourages. Other forms of gift giving are also suggested and explained without ever using the words "planned giving," "gift planning," or "deferred giving," which is extremely important to note especially in relation to the purpose of this book. [15] The Grinspoon Foundation materials describe what kinds of gifts can be made, and these are categorized according to those that can come from an estate, those that can be given "now," and those "that provide income."

Interestingly, *The Chronicle of Philanthropy* article referred to above, "How Jewish Community Groups Are Collaborating on Planned-Gift Fundraising," uses the words "planned giving" to describe the program. [16] This may be, as some of the respondents who were interviewed for this book claimed, because the writer was comfortable with the technical terminology.

There are two elements in particular that make the Life & Legacy program especially extraordinary and are key to its success. First, the Harold Grinspoon Foundation provides each community a structured four-year curriculum as well as ongoing training and mentoring. It also hosts an annual, national conference that everyone involved in Life & Legacy—staff and volunteers—is invited to attend. This gathering offers workshops and support from the national staff as well as an opportunity for participants to socialize and learn from one another.

Second, the Harold Grinspoon Foundation leadership recognizes that in order to effect change in a community, a sizable amount of time and money must be invested in order to implement a project, prove its worth, make adjustments, and realize results. Too many foundations put money into short-term grants and then are surprised when outcomes fall short of expectations.

There are other unique features that add to Life & Legacy's success—the incentive grants as well as the cooperation among agencies encouraged by the federation/foundation oversight. However, I think that the ongoing training and mentoring as well as extended timeline for implementation are the singular most extraordinary design elements.

THE ORIGINS OF LIFE & LEGACY

Harold Grinspoon, the namesake of the Foundation, was a supporter of endowment building from the beginning of his philanthropic career. I met him in the mid-1980s in his hometown of Springfield, Massachusetts, when I was hired to be the executive director of the Jewish Foundation of Greater Springfield (now the Jewish Federation and Foundation of Western Massachusetts). Even then he felt that endowment development was important, and in order to launch the Federation's effort, he financed a substantial portion of the program's budget. In addition, he created a donor-advised fund, and he and his wife, Diane Troderman, also established several restricted funds as well as an unrestricted one—all to support the local Jewish community and to ensure the success of the Federation's endowment effort. In addition to financial backing, Diane and Harold were always ready to help in any way they could, whether it was through hosting events, creating challenge grants to encourage donations, or providing advice and counsel when asked.

Harold became intrigued about spreading the idea of endowment development within Jewish federations across the country when he was introduced to a program that had been established by the Jewish Community Foundation of San Diego, California, "Create a Jewish Legacy." The key elements of that initiative were the focus on obtaining Letters of Intent as well as providing agency incentives to promote participation. In 2008 Harold hired Gail Littman, who had created the San Diego program along with Marjory Kaplan, former chief executive officer of the San Diego Jewish Community Foundation, to help him launch a similar effort in western Massachusetts. "Gail and Marjory ran the San Diego program for a few years," and its success became known within the Jewish community, explained Arlene Schiff.[17]

Gail began by creating and leading training workshops on the local level in western Massachusetts. Together with Harold she established a legacy component as part of the Harold Grinspoon Foundation Jcamp 180 program, which focused on enhancing Jewish summer camps, especially in relation to fundraising and, in particular, endowment development. Soon thereafter they created a national two-year pilot project working with Jewish federations in San Francisco, Tucson, St. Louis, and Philadelphia. Some Hillel college campus affiliates were also included at that time. Based on the success of those efforts, Life & Legacy was launched.

Some Issues

As in every large-scale project such as this one, there are issues that arise and need to be resolved. For example, Life & Legacy requires that all legacy contributions secured as part of the program be placed in an endowment, preferably that of the Jewish federation or foundation. However, this is sometimes not possible because participating local institutions have their own endowment funds, often long-standing ones, with established investment and management committees overseeing them.

In addition, some Jewish federations, like the one in South Palm Beach County, have guidelines, established before the introduction of Life & Legacy, that require realized deferred gifts below a certain amount to be placed in current operating accounts.[18] (See chapter 2.) The position of the Harold Grinspoon Foundation in these cases is that a gift can neither be defined nor counted as a true legacy if it is spent upon receipt. Arlene Schiff argues that the whole concept of endowment building is that "a gift must 'spin' off money every year and thus have an impact over time." On the other hand, she admits that some of the organizations participating in Life & Legacy claim that "their donors just don't care"[19] whether their gifts are ultimately placed in an endowment fund or not, which is a similar viewpoint to what I repeatedly heard when interviewing professional fundraising staff for this book.

Staff turnover, explained Schiff, is an issue that can undermine the success of some local programs, but that circumstance is certainly not specific to Life & Legacy. It is a problem endemic to the not-for-profit sector in general and development departments in particular.[20] Success, Schiff explained, is very much dependent on the commitment of "leadership including senior staff and the board." And that kind of commitment is not just to this specific program but also to the concept of changing the culture of philanthropy for the long term.[21] "When there is committed leadership, the program flourishes; when not, the organizations participate fully but the culture shift is not as dramatic," Schiff explained.[22]

The competition of Life & Legacy with the annual campaign is an issue for many of the communities, and Schiff readily admits that "some organizations have put their legacy effort on hold as a result of board members' fear that it will limit the amount of money they can raise for a capital or other special campaign." But the "selling point" of Life & Legacy—if there needs to be one—is easy, she claimed. "Endowments are no longer a luxury; they are part of every not-for-profit's financial stability plan and therefore, while organizations obviously have to undertake annual fundraising, they can't ignore the fact they also need to be building up their endowment."[23]

And this is Harold Grinspoon's perspective, too, and why he recognized that Life & Legacy was "an effort that was worth his investment." He explained that "endowment development is important because it is our key to securing the future of valued organizations. There is a great transfer of wealth going on from one generation to the next and the organizations that are working to capture some of this wealth are going to have greater stability than those that don't."[24]

Harold also made two additional interesting observations especially from the perspective of this book. He explained that while "there is great wealth now, we don't know if future generations will have the same capacity to give," which is indeed true. He also stated an important donor-oriented, as opposed to institutional, reason for supporting endowment development: "It is an opportunity to provide those donors, who have been the main funders of organizations for many years, the ability to think about their legacy and how they would like to be remembered."[25]

These arguments are very similar to those made in chapter 3. On the one hand, we don't know if future generations will support the organizations of today or, stated in other words, whether there will be "intergenerational equity" so that future generations have the same access to services as current recipients. Remember the James Tobin argument: "The trustees of an endowed institution are the guardians of the future against the claims of the present." And an endowment gift may be the only mechanism that a donor has to support an organization in a way that is meaningful to the contributor and, hopefully, the recipient institution—in other words, to leave a legacy.

There is another benefit to the Life & Legacy program. It has forced so many of the participating organizations to think about and create policies governing the disposition of realized, unrestricted deferred gifts. Since the program, notwithstanding some of the unique circumstances noted above, requires that the contributions resulting from Life & Legacy be deposited into a permanent endowment fund, it has compelled organizations to wrestle with the adoption of this particular policy. This is an important outcome that may or may not have been intended but is certainly a worthwhile discussion for any board.

AN ENDNOTE

Over the years, I have been a vocal naysayer about the use of Letters or Declarations of Intent programs to bring attention to as well as ensure future bequests. My opinion was based on my personal experience.

On several occasions throughout my fundraising career, people had either claimed that they had made a provision in their estate plan for the charity where I worked or actually signed what we called "Letters of Intent." Frequently, however, on the demise of the individual, no gift ever materialized. I thus became somewhat cynical about the use of these Letters as a cultivation tool, and as I stated in my 2017 book, *The Donor Lifecycle Map: A Model for Fundraising Success*, "I placed my efforts on obtaining current or deferred endowment contributions," from which, in the latter case, the donor would receive income during his or her lifetime. At least in these circumstances, real assets—not promises—would pass from the individual to the charity. While we "did have a legacy society and we included the names of people who told us that they had made a deferred gift to benefit our organization,"[26] I exerted no effort in this arena. I had been disappointed too many times.

After studying the Harold Grinspoon Foundation's Life & Legacy program, I have come to realize that the problem that I encountered was not related to the donors—although I am not letting them completely "off the hook"—but rather to the organizations that received the promise. Admittedly, I was the lead staff person in many cases and I made no specific plan to cultivate the individuals who had claimed that they had made a provision for the charitable organization in their estate plan. The policy was to accept the word of the potential donor and create what were referred to as special, often named "societies" to recognize these future gift-givers while they were alive. We never asked for documentation of a future donation nor created any kind of system whereby we would pay special attention to these people. They received invitations to events just like everyone else, but we made no particular effort to meet with them, hold special functions for them, or treat them in any way differently from others with whom we interacted.

In retrospect I can honestly state that one of the problems was resources. We just did not have enough to manage all of our cultivation efforts, but admittedly we were also unaware of what was needed in order to obtain, increase, and ensure that these future commitments became realities. It was just not a priority maybe due to a lack of understanding of what could result from a well-thought-out process.

The Harold Grinspoon Foundation Life & Legacy program not only proves that the effort is worthwhile, but it also provides a model to be replicated by other organizations—especially those with a mandate to ensure the vitality of the not-for-profit sector in their respective geographical areas such as community foundations. Corporate foundations could also duplicate the program as well as philanthropists who are committed to the long-term impact of their short-term grants. As Harold Grinspoon claims, fellow donors who "follow in his footsteps and make big investments in endowment building" would in turn "build their own legacy." But his strongest argument for creating a similar program is "the return on investment."[27]

Life & Legacy is not an initiative that should be limited to the Jewish community or by the budget of the Harold Grinspoon Foundation. The latter has proven that the model "works." It is now time for replication throughout the United States and maybe beyond given the current population of baby boomers who might appreciate and/or respond to encouragement to support their local communities and favored organizations with current and future gifts. Such commitments will have no impact on their lifestyles but could provide a legacy as well as satisfaction in the long run.

NOTES

1. https://hgf.org/.
2. https://jewishlifelegacy.org/.
3. National Update Life & Legacy, December 31, 2019. These figures were updated in an e-mail from Arlene D. Schiff, national director of Life & Legacy, to author, March 9, 2020.
4. Arlene D. Schiff, e-mail to author, February 9, 2020.
5. Jewish organizations operating within a community are eligible to participate in Life & Legacy if they agree to adhere to the guidelines of the project. Many of these institutions serve the residents of an entire geographic region whether they are Jewish or not.
6. According to Wikipedia, "a Jewish Federation is the secular primary Jewish nonprofit organization found within most metropolitan areas (or sometimes states) in North America that host a substantial Jewish community. Their broad purpose is to provide 'human services', generally, but not exclusively, to the local Jewish community" as well as to select national organizations and not-for-profit institutions in Israel. Many of these federations either house an endowment fund for long-term support or are aligned with a separate not-for-profit organization whose purpose is to ensure the long-term financial interests of the Jewish community. Whatever the structure of these entities—shared or separate not-for-profit number—they are commonly referred to as the "foundation."

7. Arlene D. Schiff, e-mail to author, March 10, 2020. A template for the plan can be found in appendix B.

8. The Harold Grinspoon Foundation guideline is $5,000 in the first of the four-year program for eighteen signed commitments; the same for the second year. Most communities offer an additional incentive of between $1,000 and $2,500 to local agencies that obtain twenty-five signed Declarations of Intent in each of these years. In the third year of the program, organizations are required to obtain four to six new Declarations of Intent (each community decides the exact number), but the emphasis is on obtaining formal assurances of a legacy gift from the Declaration signers. The Grinspoon Foundation recommends that a minimum of 50 percent of the individuals who signed the Declaration of Intent during the first two years provide legal documentation of their future gift or make an outright endowment donation. In addition in year three, the organizations must prepare and implement a stewardship plan. Individual communities can design their own incentive plans, which could include rewards for "printing testimonials, providing for the Federation/Foundation to meet once a year with [each participating] organizational board, securing more than the minimum new Letters of Intent," and more. Arlene D. Schiff, national director, Life & Legacy, interview with author, November 21, 2019, and subsequent e-mail, December 10, 2019.

9. The Harold Grinspoon Foundation, Create a Jewish Legacy, https://jewishlifelegacy.org.

10. Arlene D. Schiff, e-mail to author, December 10, 2019.

11. Arlene D. Schiff, e-mail to author, December 10, 2019.

12. Eden Stiffman, "How Jewish Community Groups Are Collaborating on Planned-Gift Fundraising," *The Chronicle of Philanthropy*, September 13, 2017.

13. Stiffman, "How Jewish Community Groups."

14. *The American Heritage Dictionary* (Boston: Houghton Mifflin Company, 1985), 722.

15. I did find the words "planned giving" in the model Life & Legacy Partnership Agreement but not anywhere else.

16. Stiffman, "How Jewish Community Groups."

17. Arlene D. Schiff, interview with author, November 21, 2019.

18. As noted in chapter 2, the Jewish Federation of South Palm Beach County spends all realized, unrestricted deferred gifts below $25,000. Some communities spend all estate gifts below $5,000. Arlene D. Schiff, interview with author, November 21, 2019.

19. Arlene D. Schiff, interview with author, November 21, 2019.

20. This was such an important issue that the Evelyn and Walter Haas Jr. Fund commissioned a study the findings from which were published in 2013, *UnderDeveloped: A National Study of Challenges Facing Nonprofit Fundraising*. Nothing seems to have changed in the interim years according to an article by Ruth McCambridge in the *Nonprofit Quarterly*, "High Nonprofit Frontline Turnover Rates Require Focus and Collective Chutzpah," January 3, 2017.

21. Evelyn and Walter Haas Jr. Fund, *UnderDeveloped: A National Study of Challenges Facing Nonprofit Fundraising*.

22. Arlene D. Schiff, interview with author, November 21, 2019.

23. Arlene D. Schiff, interview with author, November 21, 2019.

24. Arlene D. Schiff, interview with author, November 21, 2019. (Arlene Schiff interviewed Harold Grinspoon and provided his replies to my pre-submitted questions at this meeting.)

25. Arlene D. Schiff, interview with author, November 21, 2019.

26. Deborah Kaplan Polivy, *The Donor Lifecycle Map: A Model for Fundraising Success* (Nashville: CharityChannel Press, 2017), 47.

27. Arlene D. Schiff, interview with author, November 21, 2019.

Chapter Five

Who Are Endowment Donors?

Endowment donors for the most part are what writers about planned giving, charitable gift planning, and legacy giving describe as "loyals." Sagrestano and Wahlers define "loyals" as individuals "who have made fifteen or more gifts and have given in ten or more consecutive years."[1] Given that it is hard to identify who might be a prospective endowment contributor, loyalty is a good place to start.

Prospects can be narrowed down even further to include women, people without children, those with "higher education,"[2] and older individuals nearing retirement age and beyond. Adrian Sargeant, Jen Shang, and associates in their book, *Fundraising Principles and Practice*, identify "lapsed" loyal donors as prospects, too, especially if they are older. They suggest that these people may have stopped giving for any number of reasons, but if they had been ongoing contributors at one time, it would be worthwhile for fundraisers to start or continue talking to them. However, they claim, and I agree, that at some point, charities have to be careful when meeting with this older cohort because of the threat or reality of dementia or some other debilitating disease. The authors advise, "These audiences may be more vulnerable than other groups of donors because of age or illness and ensure that any bequest [or in my words endowment] fundraising is conducted sensitively and appropriately."[3] The last thing that any charity wants is a supporter's relative to claim that an organization took advantage of a family member who was ill and/or may not have understood what he or she was doing when agreeing to a contribution.

Priority setting in relation to the cultivation of potential endowment donors is important especially when there are limited fundraising resources. I think that it is probably not very productive to cultivate younger supporters because their priorities can change over time, and if they provide for a charity through a future gift such as a bequest in a will or a retirement plan designation, these are easily altered. An outright endowment contribution is obviously different and certainly worth pursuing if the opportunity arises.

When I began in the field of endowment development, "loyals" were not our focus. We concentrated on talking to the wealthy—those people who made major gifts to our organization and also those who did not make such contributions but who we believed had the means to do so. This was our modus operandi notwithstanding that people who had made what we considered "small" donations and done so loyally frequently came through the doors and made outright endowment contributions, usually in memory or in honor of a family member, or they established one or more charitable gift annuities. However, we paid little attention to these individuals and cultivated the rich or at least those who we thought had wealth. And this approach, notwithstanding that the literature advises a somewhat different emphasis, has really not changed very much since then.

Students from the Stanford University Graduate School of Business reported in the *Stanford Social Innovation Review* that their research "on the state of planned giving" (that is the terminology they use in the article) showed that "staffing structures within most organizations ignore small donors, even though they are far more numerous" than those making substantial gifts. These students write, "Planned giving personnel almost always are part of the 'major gifts' team, where they tend to adopt the toolset of that discipline: They identify top prospects, schedule in-person meetings and gradually secure commitments. This structure," they conclude, "incorrectly de-prioritizes a much larger opportunity: recruiting small-dollar donors who might include the organization in their estate planning." The students recommend, among other things, that "organizations should recognize that while small-dollar donors have significantly less disposable income for immediate giving compared to major donors, many have significant illiquid assets such as real estate, thanks to the increase in home values during the last thirty years."[4] These students clearly are looking at the California housing market, but notwithstanding that fact, these same potential donors could have appreciated holdings in the stock market or retirement funds, or they might be beneficiaries of a transfer of wealth themselves.[5]

My cursory research on *The Chronicle of Philanthropy* job site found the same thing as the Stanford students.[6] First, I learned that "Planned Giving" was the designation under "All Fundraising" that was used for endowment development—none of the other more fashionable terminology such as "gift planning" or "legacy giving" was even mentioned in terms of the headings or the actual job descriptions. I also found that the title "Planned Giving" is often combined with "major" or "principal" gift and then what appears is a job description for a joint "Planned Giving and Major Gift Officer." For example, "the successful candidate for a position as a 'Major and Planned

Giving Officer' will report to the Executive Director of Major Gifts and serve as part of the Major Gift Team." In one case, a Director of Planned Giving was "expected to make use of provided modeling and wealth screening to prospect for longtime, loyal donors with high bequest likelihood and the capacity to make seven-figure plus planned gifts." In another position, the candidate was expected to work "collaboratively with individual donors [in order] to cultivate and solicit planned and major gifts." Although one of these descriptions does refer to "loyals," only major donor loyals are the intended target population. Interestingly, when I scoured advertisements for major gift officers, as opposed to those for planned giving, I found no mention of any expectation that these people would be responsible for identifying "planned giving" prospects or any kind of deferred gift opportunities among their target audience. But just to emphasize, this was not an intense research project but rather a cursory review. Notwithstanding that fact, it was telling.

The Chronicle of Philanthropy is not alone in how it promotes endowment development positions. Individual search firms in the not-for-profit sector also list opportunities in planned giving as "Director of Planned and Major Giving" as do web-based sites such as Indeed.com.[7]

My point is not to criticize the search firms and/or not-for-profit organizations that advertise these employment opportunities, but rather to redirect the focus on endowment development prospects away from major donors and to place it on all donors who have been contributing to an institution over some significant period of time. These are the primary prospects for endowment gifts. As a matter of fact, I would claim that major donors who make endowment gifts are probably also long-term contributors, in other words, "loyals." While an individual might suddenly appear at a charitable organization and contribute what is considered by the institution to be a major gift, he or she is not likely to move from that position to endowment gift donor without some history of contributing or other kind of involvement, such as recipient of service, alumna or alumnus, volunteer, or family member of someone in these categories.

Loyalty and trust are the key factors in identifying prospects for endowment gifts—supporters who have contributed over time and are confident that the charity will do well with their monies. In an article in *The Chronicle of Philanthropy* that describes "How to Strike Gold with Endowment Gifts," the writer states that "those who give to an endowment are usually strong supporters already and want to see the institution carry on its work for years. They're often older and perhaps thinking about the legacy they want to leave." This same author states that "generally, endowment gifts are large donations and they often come in the form of planned gifts or complex assets."[8] While the endowment donations may be substantial, there is no mention in the article that the annual gifts of these contributors were similarly large. And in one case, the article describes that "more than once" residents of a senior living establishment "left a bequest to the endowment though they had never talked to development staff."[9] Again, it seems that trust and history or experience with the institution seem to be the distinguishing factors.

It appears, after reviewing so much material about planned giving and endowment development, that there are "mixed messages" coming from the field. On the one hand, the institutions and their search firm consultants are focusing on the major donor as the endowment prospect while the writers and researchers are pointing to the loyals notwithstanding the size of what is commonly referred to as the annual gift. There are those who think that endowment prospects are both loyal and major donors while Sagrestano and Wahlers claim that "less than 10 percent of identified loyal donors are rated as major gift prospects (ability to make a $100,000 gift over five years, or $20,000 per year)" in a "typical wealth screening." In other words, the people who are most likely to make an endowment gift, according to Sagrestano and Wahlers, are "off your radar and have not been actively cultivated or solicited for significant commitments to your nonprofit."[10] While those organizations looking for quick success in endowment development might subscribe to the major gift/loyal donor guideline with a few other demographic characteristics also included as noted in the beginning of this chapter (e.g., females and people without children), continuity—or number of years of giving—is the most important indicator for the purpose of priority setting in terms of prospect identification.

Greg Lassonde, a consultant on legacy giving who teaches at the Sanford Institute of Philanthropy of the John F. Kennedy University in Pleasant Hill, California, defines a "prospect" for an endowment contribution as a "long term supporter with a heart connection."[11] And continuing with this metaphor, Sagrestano and Wahlers emphasize the importance of working with the contributor until the point that the "donor has elevated the nonprofit to the status of family member and has a much greater investment in the nonprofit's success."[12] These feelings of affection do not necessarily equate with a major donor especially in terms of yearly contributions. Amy Goldman, senior director of gift planning at Massachusetts Institute of Technology, described to me the conversation she had with a graduate of the school who had never given more than approximately $100 on an annual basis and who had called to talk to her about setting up a multi-million-dollar endowment.[13] And Lassonde notes that a "misconception" about building an endowment program is that such an effort "is only for the wealthy."[14]

THE DONOR LIFECYCLE MAP AND THE ENDOWMENT DONOR

The Donor Lifecycle Map[15] is a graphic that provides a terrific framework for strategic planning for fund development—all fund development. The concept upon which the map is built is donor retention—from first gift to "ultimate" or what I refer to as the endowment contribution. The model can be used by a nonprofit organization to analyze how well it is keeping supporters over time and, then based on its findings, build a strategic plan both for the short and long term. Since the Donor Lifecycle Map is based on maintaining supporters, it is a good tool for identifying potential endowment contributors or "loyals."

The first two sectors of the Donor Lifecycle Map—first and second gift—are self-explanatory; they describe individuals who have given one and then a subsequent donation to a charitable organization. Quite naturally, the second gift sector is smaller than the first since it is somewhat impossible to retain all first-time contributors.

Second-year active—the third section on the map—is based on the concept that if someone has made two donations, then he or she is a prospect for increased engagement with the organization whose objective is to increase the donor's commitment. In my prior books, I have noted that such cultivation tools as on-site visits, face-to-face meetings, participation in committees or phonathons, event chairmanship, and so on can all be used to strengthen a

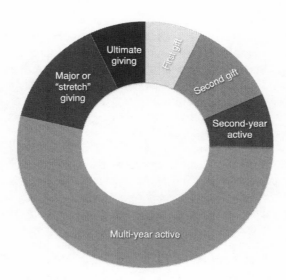

Figure 5.1.   Donor Lifecycle Map. *Courtesy of Sarah Clifton.*

contributor's support for an organization as long as these opportunities are well-planned by the not-for-profit and meaningful to the donor.[16]

Many donors, even when invited, do not want to become involved with an organization beyond contributing and thus do not move to the second-year active sector of the map. They might claim to be busy with other charities, family, or work, or they just might not be interested. However, notwithstanding such a response, the objective of the charity is to "move" second-gift donors as well as those who become second-year active to one of the next two segments on the Donor Lifecycle Map—multi-year active or major or stretch giving. The former sector is comprised of people who have made three or more gifts to an organization and according to the graphic represent almost 50 percent of all donors. The next segment—major or stretch giving—includes a smaller number of people, but their level of support is categorized as a major gift by the organization or as a stretch gift, which is determined by the donor. In other words, the "stretch" contributor feels so strongly about the organization that he or she is donating as much as possible within the constraints of personal resource availability but not at the major gift level as specified by the organization. Donors reach this sector on the map if they, too, have made three or more gifts. If not, no matter the size of the contribution, they are considered first- or second-gift supporters. Finally, the last segment of the Donor Lifecycle Map is "ultimate" giving or—as I define it—the endowment contribution.

The natural foci, using the map, for identifying endowment prospects are the two segments entitled multi-year active and major/stretch giving. For those supporters who have given over the years but not at the stretch or major gift level, the goal of the cultivation effort is not only to retain these contributions and even to increase the size of them, but more importantly in terms of this book is to move them to ultimate giving along with, of course, those people in the major/stretch segment of the map. These are the prospects for endowment contributions using the Donor Lifecycle Map as a guide—individuals who have given over time, no matter the size of their respective donations. And while three or more years of ongoing contributions is one variable for sorting donors into the two categories, multi-year active or major/stretch, I would claim that a much longer donative history has to be evident before these people become endowment prospects. On the other hand, the map provides a starting point in terms of prospect analysis, and I have used it to demonstrate to so many organizations that they have a pool of possible endowment contributors and need to create an endowment development program to harness their potential. As a matter of fact, one organization that had endowment fundraising on the so-called back burner moved it to a priority as a result of categorizing their donors according to the Donor Lifecycle Map. For those not-for-profits with endowment programs, the Donor

Lifecycle Map provides them with a visual of their prospects and demonstrates how many individuals could be making such gifts if they were asked.

Many years ago, just out of curiosity, I placed the traditional Donor Pyramid that is commonly used in creating a fundraising strategy over the Donor Lifecycle Map to determine if there was any coincidence.

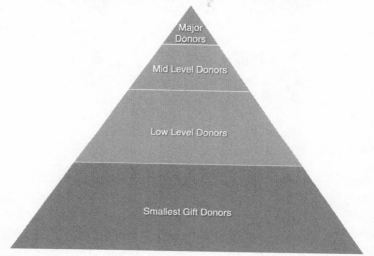

Figure 5.2. Model of a Traditional Donor Pyramid. *Courtesy of the author.*

What struck me as well as so many of the people who have seen this illustration is that the intersection of the Donor Pyramid and the Donor Lifecycle Map is at the bottom of each: on the pyramid at what is commonly referred to as the base where there are the most donors who give the smallest-size gifts and the multi-year active segment of the map where lie those who give multiple gifts but never at the major/stretch gift level. This illustration shows very dramatically that the smallest-size gift donors on the pyramid and the longest-giving donors as illustrated on the Donor Lifecycle Map coincide as prospects for endowment fundraising.

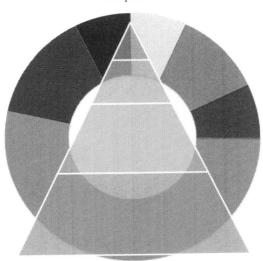

Figure 5.3.   The Intersection of the Donor Pyramid and the Donor Lifecycle Map.
Courtesy of the author.

In summary, this illustration reinforces the concept that the Donor Lifecycle Map not only is an effective tool for analyzing retention in all fundraising efforts but also is particularly useful in identifying prospects for endowment giving. In other words, retention and thus loyalty are key factors, and the longer any donor has contributed to a charitable organization, the more likely he or she will "move" to the ultimate or endowment donation notwithstanding the size of the annual gift.

I have noticed on the Internet and in articles that some writers are trying to find a place for what they refer to as planned giving on or within the traditional donor pyramid, but for the most part, their efforts really do not "work" in terms of identifying endowment prospects. For example, the graphic in one article includes planned gifts at the top, but it really makes no sense because the categories are incompatible: the bottom two rungs refer to frequency of gifts, the next to size of contributions, and finally at the top is planned giving, which is really not the primary focus of most organizations that use the Donor Pyramid for strategic planning since major gifts continue to dominate this position.[17] Nor is endowment development the natural next step for major gift donors; it is for loyal donors, some of whom may donate substantial sums.

Figure 5.4. A Variation on the Donor Pyramid. *Courtesy of the author.*

I like the next donor pyramid, which I also found on the Internet, because it shows that planned giving, or rather endowment development, can be appropriate for all donors along the pyramid—again, gift size is not the prerequisite. The difference between it and the Donor Lifecycle Map, once again, is the concept of longevity. This diagram only demonstrates that anyone can be an endowment donor; it does not refer to the concept of loyalty.[18]

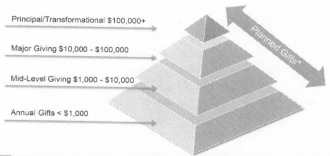

Figure 5.5. Planned Giving Prospects. *Courtesy of Lawrence Henze.*

Once the notion of loyalty is defined by choosing a relevant number of years or even number of gifts (and this will obviously vary from one organization to the next depending on the age of the institution), the quantity of donors over time, and the quality of record-keeping (which varies greatly in the not-for-profit sector), there are additional factors that can be used to identify endowment prospects. These are primarily demographic characteristics that can be applied in order to prioritize who should receive the most attention. I always start with three categories—women, older people, and those without children. Adrian Sargeant, Jen Shang, and associates in their book, *Fundraising Principles and Practice*, agree with these and add one or two more such as religion, although in their case, they are writing specifically about charitable bequests. They note that "a lot of research attention has focused on demographic factors" that "influence a person to leave a charitable bequest," and they write, "The balance of evidence suggests women are more likely to give outright bequests than men, partly, perhaps, because they are likely to live longer." Age for these authors is also a factor especially middle age and older. They recommend that fundraisers continue "to talk to donors about giving as they age,"[19] paying attention to the health-related caveat noted above.

WOMEN AS ENDOWMENT DONORS

Women have more money than ever before, and there is a consensus among professional fundraisers as well as researchers that not only are they making their own gifts but they are doing so in ways that are different than men. Many years ago a study by researchers at Wheaton College in Norton, Massachusetts, found that women were most likely to use bequests, saw giving from the perspective of "emotional freedom," and had "a passion for the mission" of the organizations that they supported.

Men, on the other hand, according to the author of the study, Marjorie Houston, were inclined to make outright gifts that reflected a desire for "power, influence and recognition." Houston concluded that men were more interested "about the transaction and less about the mission."[20]

Not much has changed in the intervening years. Sagrestano and Wahlers write that "women are focused on giving money based on their values and desire to transform society, while men continue to focus more on capital projects."[21] In a 2018 study published by Fidelity Charitable Gift Fund, entitled "Women and Giving: The Impact of Generation and Gender on Philanthropy," it was reported that women "are more concerned than men about outliving their resources, even when those resources are substantial,"[22] and thus an endowment gift—either one through a bequest in a will or that provides some kind of income stream—"may be more attractive to a woman than a man."[23]

"Women's motivations for giving have remained fairly constant over time," reported Andrea Pactor, the associate director of the Women's Philanthropy Institute at the Lilly School of Philanthropy, in her article, "Women's Motivations for Charitable Giving: Constant or Changing over 30 Years?" She writes that women are more likely than men to cite personal experiences with an organization; their own or public knowledge of the organization; and the organization's connection to their family, to their friends, or to themselves as factors that influence their giving decisions. And Pactor adds that in relation to "high net worth donors," "women are significantly more likely than men to have volunteered for a charitable organization." Like so many others, she concludes that "empathy for others drives women's motivations for giving whereas for men, giving is often more about self-interest. Because women are socialized into more helping, nurturing and caring roles from an early age, these behaviors become ingrained and become the basis for many of their actions, including philanthropy."[24] The Fidelity study also reports that this socialization process is really no different whether describing millennials or boomers. "Millennial women," like boomers, "are more likely to lead with their hearts."[25]

A quick look at the subject of "women and endowment giving" on the Internet results in countless references to women's foundations, giving circles, and affinity groups and their relationship to a panoply of not-for-profit organizations, even the Boy Scouts![26] These institutions recognize the importance of female donors and their journey around the Donor Lifecycle Map to "ultimate" or endowment giving. The women's groups have a variety of names such as Women's Leadership and Philanthropy Affinity Group (Washington and Lee University)[27] and Queen of Hearts Women's Fund (Tahoe Truckee Community Foundation). Some are established to support specific programs for female athletes, such as the Women Behind the Women Scholarship Endowment (University of North Dakota).[28] What is significant is the large number of them and the simultaneous recognition of the importance of women as current and potential endowment donors.

The purpose of these women's funds and groups, no matter the charitable entity under whose auspice they operate or if they are independent, is to involve women early in the giving process in order to ultimately secure larger and more frequent annual as well endowment donations. This was an important lesson I learned when writing *The Donor Lifecycle Map: A Model for Fundraising Success*. Professionals in community foundations explained to me that they, too, need a "donor pipeline" just as other organizations and giving circles often provide them with a vehicle to introduce contributors to their charitable organizations.[29]

It appears that the difference between men and women as endowment prospects is well recognized by not-for-profit institutions in that a parallel search for "men and endowment giving" on the Internet resulted in almost no mention of specifically men's affinity groups. I found primarily generic references to endowment development—almost nothing explicit to men especially when compared to women. This may be that men are not seen as a new pool of potential donors. They have historically served on boards and made philanthropic decisions and therefore charities see no need to address them in any way that is different from what has been their traditional approach.

It is interesting to note that there are two somewhat conflicting messages that are reflected in the literature about women and philanthropy in general and endowment giving in particular. On the one hand, the fundraising field acknowledges that women have more assets than ever before because they are earning and inheriting increasing amounts while also living longer on average than their husbands if they are married. On the other hand, in spite of this knowledge, the not-for-profit organizations that seek endowment gifts have not done much to address women differently than male prospects and donors except maybe in the case of using these specific women-only funds to attract female contributors.

For example, writers like Andrea Pactor state that not-for-profit organizations have yet to fully comprehend the power of women as endowment donors and still place primary focus on the male in any relationship. She writes, "While women donors are not waiting in line to lead and to give," they are "stepping boldly into their philanthropy," but at the same time, "far fewer nonprofits are acknowledging the changing philanthropic landscape and actively engaging women in ways that appeal to them."[30] In a *Chronicle of Philanthropy* article, a similar message is communicated: "Traditionally, we always defaulted to the idea that the husband was the donor. . . . Now you really have to be careful because it can be the wife, and philanthropy is done separately as often as it is done as a couple."[31]

There is acknowledgment in the field that things are changing. In an article, "Why Less Is More: 5 Trends in Planned Giving and Endowment Building," it is clearly stated that it is "less about old, white men," and "smart development officers cultivate both husbands *and* wives; women, increasingly in executive positions, make substantial incomes in today's economy. And women (on average) outlive men by 3.7 years, so the wife may be the member of the couple making planned giving decisions."[32]

It is as if everyone in the field recognizes that women have more money than ever before and may be even more philanthropic than men in relation to endowment contributions, but somehow the development offices cannot make the leap to create different kinds of approaches for females than males, again, except maybe in the case of the women-focused funds. Debra Mesch, former director of the Women's Philanthropy Institute and professor of philanthropic studies at Indiana University's Lilly Family School of Philanthropy, says it clearly in an interview:

> When I do speaking engagements around the country, I'm always amazed by the number of women who say they feel either ignored or insulted by nonprof-

its that don't seem to understand that they are the ones making the decisions in their households about charitable giving. Many of them also tell me they are much more interested in engaging their families and children in philanthropy than their husbands are. And the implications of both those things for practitioners and nonprofit leaders are obvious: If you don't understand how to engage women donors, you're going to leave a lot of money on the table. [33]

It seems that the nonprofit sector is not very different than Wall Street. In an article entitled "Women to Wall Street: Are You Listening?" the author, MP Dunleavey, writes, "Imagine that you work for a financial company. You've plowed through stacks of research showing that women—who are increasingly educated and affluent—could be a big source of revenue for you. Now what?" She continues, "If you're thinking that it can't be that hard to bring female customers in the door, let me bring you up to speed: Women control trillions of dollars of wealth in the United States, yet as clients, they pose a challenge to Wall Street's traditional way of doing business." She concludes, "Finance has a long and hidebound history, and it may well be necessary to take a traditional approach to get the ball rolling faster. 'It's a multifaceted challenge . . . and it will take creating the right training and incentive structures to shift advisers' mind-sets and behavior.'"[34]

The traditional incentive structure in the not-for-profit world, how much is brought in any one year—the "One Number" as Steve Meyers calls it—certainly won't work in the field of endowment development where gifts are often not realized for some time in the future. Maybe, like Wall Street, we in the charitable world will have to think differently about how we relate to female endowment prospects and how we train our employees and board members to address them. Many fundraisers have recognized the potential of women as endowment donors and modified their approaches to them. However, these articles and quotes demonstrate that these changes are certainly not universal within the field.

THE CHILDLESS

A natural demographic for endowment development is the childless whether in relation to the never married or the couple with no children. Endowment fundraising professionals have always recognized that if someone falls into this category, there is a substantial chance that he or she is a good prospect for a gift. Research on planned giving and charitable estate planning has confirmed this fact. According to Adrian Sargeant, Jen Shang, and associates in their book, *Fundraising Principles and Practice*, "The most comprehensive data on who in the United States leaves legacies comes from Russell James's analysis of the Health and Retirement Study. The most influential factor James identifies is the presence or absence of children and grandchildren." Sargeant and Shang report that "when donors had a will or trust, childless people were five times more likely to have included a charitable gift than those with grandchildren." They suggest, of course, "the importance of appropriately gathering data on the presence or absence of children in order to understand whether bequest giving might be right for supporters."[35] The easiest way to do that is probably through face-to-face conversations with potential donors or through information gathering from other contributors or people involved with the organization.

AGE AS A FACTOR IN ENDOWMENT GIVING

Age is an interesting variable in relation to endowment development, and there are multiple opinions as to who are the best prospects within this demographic. Sagrestano and Wahlers created charts where they identify different age-related cohorts and assign them labels, "Traditionalists," "Leading Boomers," "Trailing Boomers," and including "Millennials." They emphasize the importance of paying attention to the "New Philanthropists"— those who have come after the "Traditionalists," the last of whom "reached the retirement age of sixty-five" in 2010. These "New Philanthropists" are the "Leading Boomer and the generations that follow," and each of them needs to be approached in different ways according to these authors.[36]

For me it's a lot to think about and remember. As far as endowment gifts are concerned, I would just state that baby boomers are the priority especially those sharing the characteristics described in the preceding paragraphs (e.g., loyals, women, and childless). The consensus in the field also points to baby boomers. The headlines are all the same: "Baby Boomers Poised to Give $8 Trillion, Study Says"[37]; "Philanthropy's Missing Trillions"[38]; and "Charities Vie for Boomers' Planned Gifts."[39]

While many writers refer to the anticipated role that baby boomers will play in endowment giving, myself included, these are not just opinions; data support these conclusions. Sargeant, Shang, and their associates note that while *Giving USA* numbers have shown that "overall giving accounted for by bequests has remained remarkably constant over time. . . . The good news for bequest fundraisers is that their market will expand dramatically in the coming years." They attribute this rise "to the passing of the Baby Boom generation (that is, those individuals born between 1946 and 1964)." The authors then explain that while this generation will be living longer and spending "significant sums on health and nursing care," "even accounting for this expenditure . . . forecasters are predicting a significant bulge in the transfer of wealth."

Sargeant, Shang, and their associates then suggest that along with this great sum of money, there "is likely to be an increasing proportion of people remembering not-for-profits with a gift in their wills." They refer back to the studies of Russell James mentioned above where he "finds a growing trend toward including charitable bequests in estate plans with the percentage of US [United States] over-55s with a will or trust including a bequest increasing from 8.28 percent to 10.12 percent between 1998 and 2008." The authors conclude that "offering Boomers the opportunity to continue their support of their favorite causes after their deaths is likely to provide a substantial opportunity to grow bequest income during the middle decades of the 20th century." But, they say, it won't be easy and "not-for-profits ideally need to invest in their bequest fundraising programs now."[40]

Notwithstanding the timeline of Sargeant and his colleagues, it is certainly not too late to focus on the transfer of wealth and the opportunity to encourage endowment giving. This is exactly the route that Harold Grinspoon has taken through his foundation's support of the Life & Legacy program. Harold was very clear when asked why he funded the initiative; he stated that he wanted to ensure that charitable organizations take advantage of the huge amount of money that would be transferred over the coming years.

WEALTH

What about wealth? The emphasis on planned giving and major gifts as complementary efforts suggests that wealth is an important factor in endowment development, at least according to some fundraisers. On the other hand, not so say some authors as well as experts in the field. For the most complex gifts—charitable trusts of all kinds—it is acknowledged that these are for the most wealthy, especially because they "tend to be comfortable and familiar with the notions of long-term capital investment and endowment—it is what they do with their own money."[41] And I think that Steven Meyers's concept of "Personalized Philanthropy," where individuals donate while they are alive the projected annual spending rate of a future endowment gift, assumes wealth or, as he says, "just modest wealth."[42] This is why the senior philanthropic advisors at St. Jude Children's Research Hospital in Memphis, Tennessee, are addressing "High Net Wealth individuals" for "blended gifts" like those described by Meyers. These professionals "have actual revenue goals," as it was explained to me.[43]

However, as I have written and others have corroborated, it is much easier to count in terms of fundraising performance a complex endowment gift in which monies are received in any given year than promises that might not be realized for decades. "Development leaders prefer to emphasize areas where they can show clear success to their boss or their board," and for the most part, unless some of Meyers's suggestions are adopted in terms of "metrics"[44] for planned gifts or counting and giving credit for projected commitments,[45] then the wealthy will always receive the most attention.

Wealth is an important issue. Think back to the Donor Lifecycle Map. The major gift donor's next step is the ultimate or endowment gift. And while this may be a small sector in the entire map compared to others, about 25 percent in terms of total number of donors in the model, actual maps from innumerable organizations demonstrate that this is the segment from which the most money is raised—but that is in terms of annual gifts. As the Stanford Business School students conclude, "Small-dollar donors (and even non-donors, who are fans of an organization but have not donated) make up the lion's share of planned giving at most organizations." However, this finding relates to bequests. "In fact," they write, "our research suggests a dynamic in which the most frugal donors are also lifelong savers who are well-positioned to give the largest bequests."[46]

But it's not all about bequests. Those donors who contribute the maximum allowed for charitable gifts from a retirement plan[47]—$100,000 of the Required Minimum Distributions (RMD)—also fall into the category of wealthy since they have sufficient means to neither need nor want these payouts and prefer not to pay the income tax due on them. I once sat on a panel with such a donor who explained to the audience how he took the maximum RMD payout of $100,000 and donated it one year to his alma mater and the next to a local not-for-profit organization. Over ten years he had built up named endowment funds of $500,000 at each of these institutions and planned to continue the practice as long as he was alive. His goal was to have two $1 million named endowment funds! After his death, he explained, whatever money was left in the retirement plan would be divided equally between the two charities, and he hoped that even larger endowment funds would result.[48]

There is no way of denying that the wealth of the donor is an important consideration in endowment building. However, all of the information related in this chapter points to another factor that is more significant and that is loyalty. As Amy Goldman states, "Frequently, the decision to make a provision in the will comes after a donor has made regular gifts to MIT for some time."[49] And as Adrian Sargeant and his colleagues write, "The bulk of the literature and support available to planned giving fundraisers concentrates on the technical aspects of that area of fundraising," and not on the "human dynamic."[50] They continue that "several surveys of planned givers, and of the largest givers in the United States, point to the fact that the work of the organization and the desire to make a difference to that are far more important."[51]

Donors who establish endowment funds are usually not new to the organizations to which they contribute; they have been involved over time through donating and often volunteering or in some other way have developed into a loyal supporter. Of course if they also have wealth, then it goes without saying, theirs could be a contribution of great impact.

NOTES

1. Brian M. Sagrestano and Robert E. Wahlers, *Getting Started in Charitable Gift Planning: Your Guide to Planned Giving* (Nashville: CharityChannel Press, 2016), 57.
2. Russell N. James III, Mitzi K. Lauderdale, and Cliff A. Robb, "The Growth of Charitable Estate Planning among Americans Nearing Retirement," *Financial Services Review* 18, no. 2 (January 2009): 141–156.
3. Adrian Sargeant, Jen Shang, and Associates, *Fundraising Principles and Practice*, 2nd ed. (Hoboken, NJ: John Wiley and Sons, 2017), 473.
4. Jennifer Xia and Patrick Schmitt, "Philanthropy's Missing Trillions," *Stanford Social Innovation Review*, October 16, 2017, https://cdn.ymaws.com/www.yorkbar.com/resource/resmgr/leave_a_legacy/Philanthropy_Article.pdf.
5. When I served on the board of a small private school, the staff called me one day and asked that I participate in a meeting with potential donors. It seemed that two sisters who were each single with no children were the recipients of a major portion of their never-married brother's estate. He, too, had no children. These women came to the school because they realized that they did not need the money and they wanted to contribute it to our as well as other institutions.
6. https://www.philanthropy.com/jobs/.
7. https://www.indeed.com/jobs?q=Planned%20Giving&vjk=eacab1cef980d908.
8. Drew Lindsay, "How to Strike Gold with Endowment Gifts," *The Chronicle of Philanthropy*, December 2017, 38.
9. Lindsay, "How to Strike Gold."
10. Sagrestano and Wahlers, *Getting Started*, 57.
11. Greg Lassonde, Presentation at the Sanford Institute of Philanthropy at John F. Kennedy University, Oakland, 2019 Fundraising Academy, September 26–27, 2019.
12. Sagrestano and Wahlers, *Getting Started*, 9.
13. Amy Goldman, conversation with author, December 4, 2019.
14. Lassonde, Presentation at the Sanford Institute of Philanthropy, slide #22.
15. Sarah Clifton, http://www.101fundraising.org/2011/12/the-donor-lifecycle map. I originally found the Donor Lifecycle Map on the 101fundraising blog. It was created by Sarah Clifton who works for international not-for-profit organizations based in the Netherlands. I am profoundly indebted to her because I have used this model in most of my work since I came across it.
16. Deborah Kaplan Polivy, *Donor Cultivation and the Donor Lifecycle Map: A New Framework for Fundraising* (Hoboken, NJ: John Wiley and Sons, 2014), and *The Donor Lifecycle Map: A Model for Fundraising Success* (Nashville: CharityChannel Press, 2017).
17. Amy Quinn, "The Fund Raising Pyramid and The Donor Life-Cycle: Find Your Supporters Wherever They Are," *Forward Together*, February 8, 2013. Several models of donor pyramids are illustrated in this article.
18. Lawrence Henze, J.D., "Climbing the Donor Pyramid: Transitional and Major Giving," 2016, http://www.blackbaud.com/company/resources/whitepapers/whitepapers.aspx.
19. Sargeant and Shang, *Fundraising Principles and Practice*, 473.
20. Marjorie A. Houston, "Women and Philanthropy—Values, Vision and Voice," Wheaton College.
21. Sagrestano and Wahlers, *Getting Started*, 63.
22. Fidelity Charitable Gift Fund, "Women and Giving: The Impact of Generation and Gender on Philanthropy," 2017; Lilly Family School of Philanthropy, Women's Philanthropy Institute, "Women Give 18: Transmitting Generosity to Daughters and Sons," 2018.
23. Sagrestano and Wahlers, *Getting Started*, 53.

24. Andrea Pactor, "Women's Motivations for Charitable Giving: Constant or Changing over 30 Years?" February 21, 2019, http://blog.philanthropy.iupui.edu/2019/02/21/womens-motivations-for-charitable-giving-constant or-changing-over-30.

25. Fidelity Charitable Gift Fund, "Women and Giving," 3.

26. https://www.lhcscouting.org/about-us/giving/endowment-giving.

27. https://www.wlu.edu/give/endowment-giving/.

28. http://www.ndchampionsclub.com/wbw.

29. Polivy, *The Donor Lifecycle Map*, 82.

30. Pactor, "Women's Motivations for Charitable Giving."

31. Nicole Wallace, "Charities Vie for Boomers' Planned Gifts," *The Chronicle of Philanthropy*, November 8, 2015.

32. Benefactor Group, "Why Less is More: 5 Trends in Planned Giving and Endowment Building," 2020.

33. PND by Candid, June 28, 2016.

34. MP Dunleavey, "Women to Wall Street: Are You Listening?" *The New York Times*, July 12, 2014.

35. Sargeant and Shang, *Fundraising Principles and Practice*, 471.

36. Sagrestano and Wahlers, *Getting Started*, 58.

37. Maria DiMento, "Baby Boomers Poised to Give $8 Trillion, Study Says," *The Chronicle of Philanthropy*, October 22, 2015.

38. Xia and Schmitt, "Philanthropy's Missing Trillions."

39. Wallace, "Charities Vie for Boomers' Planned Gifts."

40. Sargeant and Shang, *Fundraising Principles and Practice*, 464–467.

41. Sargeant and Shang, *Fundraising Principles and Practice*, 511.

42. Steven L. Meyers, e-mail to author, May 9, 2020.

43. This interviewee chose to remain anonymous, but information on St. Jude's blended gifts can be found at https://www.stjude.org/give/planned-giving/imact-major-gift.html.

44. Xia and Schmitt, "Philanthropy's Missing Trillions."

45. Steven L. Meyers, *Personalized Philanthropy: Crash the Fundraising Matrix* (Nashville: CharityChannel Press, 2015), 100–105.

46. Xia and Schmitt, "Philanthropy's Missing Trillions."

47. Rules for various kinds of retirement plans are different. See Judith Ward, "Qualified Charitable Donations—A Great Gift For Unneeded RMDs," *Forbes*, Oct 29, 2019.

48. These rules have changed for the year 2020 as a result of the Coronavirus Aid, Relief, and Economic Security Act, or CARES Act. "Most donors will not have a required minimum distribution from their retirement plan in 2020. Minimum distributions will not be required from IRAs, 401(k)s, 403(b)s and most other defined contribution plans maintained by an employer for individuals. . . . However, required minimum distributions that would have had to start in 2020 don't have to start until 2021, including distributions from defined benefit pension plans and 457 plans. This change will dampen somewhat the incentive for a donor to make a qualified charitable distribution (QCD) from her IRA in 2020. Even so, making a QCD this year will still allow itemizers and non-itemizers alike to direct up to $100,000 from their IRA to charities in a tax efficient manner." https://info.pgcalc.com/cares-act.

49. Massachusetts Institute of Technology, "A World of Difference," *Corridor*, Fall 2018, 5.

50. Sargeant and Shang, *Fundraising Principles and Practice*, 514.

51. Sargeant and Shang, *Fundraising Principles and Practice*, 515.

Chapter Six

Welcome to the Office of the Chief Legacy Officer

Figure 6.1.   Welcome to the Office of the Chief Legacy Officer. *Courtesy of the author*.

A while ago I was having breakfast with a colleague who had recently assumed a new position. I asked for her business card so that I could update her contact information on my devices. She gave me the card and I made an audible gasp when I read her new title, "chief legacy officer." I quickly asked, "What is that and how do people react when they see it?" She replied that it was her boss's idea and while she did originally protest, he was adamant about the new designation in place of the former one—senior vice president of the foundation. She and I both agreed that the old title made much more sense and was easy to understand. She also commented that there were people who had asked her about the title and what it meant.

"I don't want to talk to people about it," she replied. "I want to spend time on how I can help them accomplish what they want to do." I thought, but people have to understand your title in order to pick up the telephone to ask you questions or make an appointment.

At the time of that get-together, I thought that the title—chief legacy officer—was silly. Now, after conducting research for this book and talking to many people, I am not so sure. Maybe it does make sense.

Greg Lassonde in his consulting practice recommends the title "chief legacy officer" to all of his endowment development clients, one of whom, Mark Jones, director of legacy giving at Mills College in Oakland, California, explained how commonsense it was and I found him quite convincing. He claimed that the title is "user friendly. It is a conversation starter. It is less threatening and less technical and is certainly less ominous than Director of Planned Giving." He told me that notwithstanding that he is an attorney by profession, he rarely signs his letters with either a "J.D. or Esquire" because he wants to be "donor friendly," and those words might intimidate a potential contributor.[1]

Figure 6.2. *Courtesy of the author.*

I arranged a telephone interview with the boss of my colleague and asked why he had chosen the title chief legacy officer, and his answer was somewhat different from that of Mark Jones. He replied that the title refers to "today and tomorrow" and appeals to and resonates with donors who "don't want to give money just for tomorrow but they want to think creatively today." When I asked why he did not choose the title "chief endowment officer," he said that "it was outdated and the new title, chief legacy officer, suggests a rebuilding and rethinking for the twenty-first century."

Chief legacy officer is still somewhat unique in terms of titles in the field, but if we think about why people make endowment gifts, it is usually to ensure that an organization is not only maintained but also healthy in the future, and the individuals who contribute these funds have some kind of connection to and believe in the institution. The word "legacy" suggests that linkage and commitment as well as leaving something behind.

Mark Jones refers to it as part of a person's "autobiography." He explained, "When we ask people to consider making a 'legacy' gift to Mills, we ask them to recognize what an important part of their life was represented by their time [here] and to honor that time in their lives by setting up a legacy gift."[2] On the other hand, Jones acknowledges that not all realized, unrestricted gifts are put into the permanent endowment, which creates a question as to whether or not they are in fact a "legacy" through which a donor is remembered.

The title "chief legacy officer" is not unique to the not-for-profit sector. It is described on a website for a commercial firm Family Wealth Coach, where the question is asked, "Do you have a Chief Legacy Officer?" According to the website, this person is someone who deals with "values and vision." The position is explained as follows: a "Chief Legacy Officer is to values and vision what a CEO is to executive decisions and a CFO is to financial decisions." The caption for the position is "Conversation, Family, Heirs, Planning, Values."[3]

This description makes sense in the charitable world, too. In terms of endowment gifts, isn't this what it's all about? The chief legacy officer is the person who ensures the future through working with donors to honor their values in a way that reflects a long-term vision and therefore future impact on an institution. In addition, conversations with contributors often take into consideration family members.

While the title "chief legacy officer" is seemingly new to the not-for-profit fundraising sector, over the years we have profusely created "legacy societies" to acknowledge donors who have included charitable organizations in their estate plans. We also tell prospects that one purpose for establishing an endowment gift it to leave a personal legacy. On the other hand, we rarely come across the title "chief legacy officer" within a fundraising office. And while we constantly refer to money or property that is left through a will or trust as a legacy, maybe the title chief legacy officer is not sufficiently expansive to include all of the ways in which an individual can make a future or current endowment gift. But then again, in today's usage, according to Merriam-Webster, a legacy is something "transmitted by or received from an ancestor or predecessor or from the past." The dictionary also states that currently "the word is used much more broadly" and therefore it could apply to the work we do in endowment development.[4]

If we agree, as I suggest in chapter 5, that endowment donors have strong connections to a not-for-profit organization and these are often emotional or, as Sagrestano and Wahlers claim, the contributor "has elevated the nonprofit to the status of family member,"[5] then "legacy officer" may be an inviting and appropriate title for the person responsible for endowment development. It is surely better than director of planned giving or even director of planned and major giving, which, hopefully I have successfully argued, make no sense from two perspectives. First, endowment donors are often not "major" but rather loyal, and second, "planned giving," as so many have stated, is a "technical" term used by professionals in the field but not at all inviting to nor understood by potential donors and probably board members, too.

When I interviewed David Chused at Brandeis University, he explained that "what does and does not qualify as a 'planned gift' is ultimately in the eye of the beholder. That is, there is no real uniform industry understanding as to precisely what 'planned giving' or planned gifts are and that, in the end, the terms often mean different things to different people." He continued, "Some people view planned giving as being limited to gifts that are completed today—but are not realized by the charity until some point in the future. These gifts would include things like transfers to charitable remainder trusts, the 'purchase' of a charitable gift annuity or naming a charity under the terms of a will. Others take a more expansive view of what planned giving means." He placed himself at "the far end of the spectrum" and stated that he "prefers the broadest definition of the term planned gift." In his view, "a planned gift includes any contribution that requires some additional thought on the part of the donor and has consequences which extend beyond simply being eligible to claim a charitable income tax deduction. In short this would include the transfer of anything other than a straight, currently usable gift of cash."[6]

It appears that while the field in many cases is aware of the shortcomings in the language related to the subject of endowment development or in its preferred terminology, "planned giving," it is not making a lot of change. Some organizations have modified what they call these departments and the titles within, but their descriptive language is still the same. For example, I found several institutions using the words "gift and endowment planning" to describe these fundraising departments, and I do think this better reflects the goal of endowment building, but when I actually reviewed the description of these offices, they are top-heavy with the words "planned gifts."[7]

I also looked at the titles that were held by the professionals responsible for the Life & Legacy program of the Harold Grinspoon Foundation and found that there is little consistency among them except in those cases when Life & Legacy is the only assignment of the person in charge. In that case the title always includes the words Life & Legacy along with another label such as "coordinator," "manager," or even "coach." In these instances the role of the individual holding the portfolio is very clear.

However, when the Life & Legacy program is one of many responsibilities of the individual assigned to oversee the initiative, the titles vary and include "endowment development manager," "director of foundation development," "philanthropy and gift planning advisor," and more. The most common one, however, is "director of planned giving and endowment(s)," which I assume, or at least hope, indicates a recognition that these gifts would eventually be deposited into a permanent endowment fund. No one responsible for the Life & Legacy program, at the time of writing this book, is named director of planned giving alone nor of planned and major gifts, and that fact tells me that the goal of endowment building is primary and that major gifts and endowment development are not seen as responsibilities inexorably intertwined.

I have not related all of the titles that I found for individuals working in the field of endowment fundraising. Some of them, after looking at the job descriptions, really make no sense and reflect a lack of understanding of what is even entailed in this particular endeavor. For example, one was called "director of planned giving and estates," and the person in charge, according to the job description, would hold "primary responsibility for supporting the organization's long-term financial strength by promoting gifts of bequests, charitable gift annuities, charitable remainder and lead trusts, endowments, life insurance and similar gifts that reflect legacy planning and deferred giving opportunities."[8] Since the word "endowments" is listed along with all the mechanisms by which someone can in fact create an endowment fund, and life insurance is an asset, not a mechanism for giving, my assumption is the organization is really not clear about the function in the first place. The tools and the disposition are not separate in this description but one and the same. Doug White described this phenomenon to me in an e-mail: "An endowed fund is often the *result* of the planned or outright gift. A cause leads to an effect, but that hardly makes them the same thing. (We often see another confusion in marketing materials, by the way. My pet peeve is confusing assets with vehicles. Life insurance, for example, is an asset. A remainder trust is a vehicle. Stock is an asset. And so forth. A component of one feeds the component in the other, but they are different concepts.)" (emphasis in the original).[9]

I have also found other titles such as vice president for planned giving and endowment stewardship as well as director of gift planning and director of development and planned gifts. The Fund Raising School at Indiana University includes in the notebook for registrants of its Planned Giving course a "proposed position description" of a person whose title is "Director of Planned Gift Development."[10] The focus of this person in a "prospect development flowchart" is major gifts and special gifts, downward on a donor pyramid to "donor of record."[11] The workbook recommends that any incumbent for the position begin a search for "the right" prospects among "major and special gift individuals."[12]

When I began this book, I had planned to advocate for the title "chief endowment officer" or something similar where the word "endowment" would be included as the primary functional responsibility. I thought such a designation would be very clear to donors and institutions alike. It wasn't a complicated title nor off-putting to prospects.

However, now that I have learned that so many organizations do not place their realized, unrestricted deferred gifts into an endowment and some even use the funds as soon as they are received, I cannot honestly advocate for such a title unless the institution is in fact going to deposit the money that is raised through the office into the permanent endowment or, as a default, the quasi-endowment when not specifically directed by a donor. I did find a job opening for a "chief endowment officer," and the description of the organization searching for the candidate stated quite clearly that the "philanthropy team is structured to include both an Annual Fund and an Endowment group." Moreover, when I looked at the website of this institution, while the words "planned giving" are used, the language to describe the department states that its purpose is to provide the donor with "the opportunity to establish a legacy" through the creation of an endowment fund.[13] Nice and understandable.

It could be that so many of the titles in the area of endowment development are unclear or not donor friendly because our fundraising nomenclature across the board shares similar ambiguous characteristics. For example, what does an Office of Institutional Advancement communicate to a contributor? Its premise is that the institution is of primary importance and certainly not the donor. What about another common title, Development Office? As one writer quite deftly stated: "What is the responsibility of the development office, which is such an odd name for the fundraising arm of a school? What is even being developed? Film? Land? Isn't the role of this office to ask for donations?"[14]

The American Committee for the Weizmann Institute of Science, with which Steven Meyers "crashed the fundraising matrix," uses the title "Financial Resource Development." That's a little clearer. At least we know what is being "developed."

In a *Chronicle of Philanthropy* article, Debra Blum, the writer, explains that "Weizmann doesn't run a conventional annual-giving campaign or split its fundraisers among annual-, major-and planned-giving departments. Five years ago [prior to the publication of the article], it scuttled its planned-giving program, creating instead a Center for Personalized Philanthropy, with a focus on blending gifts." Blum quotes the former chief executive officer of Weizmann's fundraising group, "This is the opposite of hit-and-run philanthropy. We take a look at the lifelong value of a donor and what their lifetime goals are for making an impact." And then Blum quotes Meyers, who describes the way in which the Weizmann fundraising department operates: "Because there are no walls between annual gifts and planned gifts and capital gifts and endowment gifts, we all could build a relationship with the donor like it was one extended conversation over the years."[15] And returning to the subject of chapter 5, "Who Are Endowment Donors?," another Weizmann fundraising executive states, "the best prospects are current donors. 'We appreciate every contribution, especially because in a life span of a donor you don't know where things will end up.'"[16]

Stacy B. Sulman, J.D., vice president for personalized philanthropy and legal affairs at the American Committee for the Weizmann Institute, who worked closely with Meyers and now heads the department, admits to "struggling" to find the appropriate language to describe what they do. She stated that she is now frequently using the term "gift planning."[17] She described how the fundraising team operates: "We concentrate on assets and how people can plan their gifts based on their assets. In gift planning we focus on how to structure the gift."[18]

She also explained that one key to the success of the Weizmann Institute's fundraising program is the "open boundaries of communication between departments. We work together as a team on gift planning," which she defines as "finding the right tool and the right timing for the donor. My job is to help all of the team to make these gifts happen."[19]

While this description of the Weizmann Institute's operation may seem somewhat ideal, and it probably is when compared to a lot of other development departments, *The Chronicle of Philanthropy* article, when describing the Weizmann methodology, notes that there is a focus both on the wealthy and on the first-time donor. One goal is "to get more donors on the rolls, even at low levels." In 2015 Weizmann began testing small online crowdfunding campaigns supporting research projects in medicine, the environment, space exploration, and other fields: "A campaign [in that year] to support brain and Alzheimer's research quickly raised $12,000 from 38 donors, more than half of them newcomers to the organization."[20]

So does the title of the department in which endowment gifts are raised and maybe all fundraising occurs really matter or is this just a meaningless discussion? I think it's an important issue because the people whom I interviewed agreed that the donor must feel welcome and the professional fundraisers need to work together and not in silos. They also all stated that while the term "planned giving" is really just nomenclature specific to professionals in the field, it is not welcoming to the donor nor really understood by him or her. And most importantly, what I have learned—and it has been reiterated time and again in both my interviews as well as in the literature—is that donors at every level want to know that their gifts will have an impact on the organizations to which they contribute.

So what do I propose? Maybe a Department of Philanthropic Impact wherein all donations—no matter the size—are recognized for their importance and contribution to the mission of the institution. Various not-for-profit organizations have realized the value of demonstrating to donors—all of them—the consequence of their gifts and are therefore creating what are called "donor impact statements." I am not writing about measuring impact per se such as return on investment (ROI) since such data are not only often misleading but extraordinarily hard to identify and calculate especially in the field of human services. I am proposing that in order to become increasingly donor friendly and responsive to individuals whose gifts might grow larger over the years, a title including the word "impact" might make a lot more sense than the Office of Institutional Advancement.

The *Chronicle of Philanthropy* reports that "It's Almost a Requirement Now to Tell Donors the Impact of Their Gifts,"[21] and even students write that notwithstanding the low level of their donations, they want to know how they are used by the recipient organization. "I wanted my small donation to 'count' for something, versus the 50 bucks here and there for other good causes," one states.[22] St. Jude Children's Research Hospital asks its donors to "Make A Lasting Impact." The website to which the contributor is referred includes the words "Impact giving," and, notwithstanding that it refers to planned and major gifts, there is also a place on this site where even a smaller-size contribution can be made although the reader has to scroll down very far to find it![23]

Steven Meyers in his book, *Personalized Philanthropy*, repeatedly uses the word "impact" to describe the goal of endowment donors. He recommends that fundraisers "try rewriting the scripts you use with donors and colleagues. Ask, 'how could we make greater impact and start it sooner?'"[24] He also claims that the work of charities is "to translate that wealth into social impact."[25] And he uses such phrases as "increased impact" and "greater impact"[26] throughout his book when describing different gifting models.

I asked several people whom I interviewed what they thought about the title Office of Philanthropic Impact. They were all quite supportive, and David Chused at Brandeis University stated that he liked it "because it takes into consideration the audience and what it cares about." He continued that he thought the title would "likely resonate with the donor and appeal to a donor to make a difference."[27] Stacy Sulman at the Weizmann Institute commented, "It's an interesting idea." She continued, "[I] struggle to find a name that works internally and with donors."[28]

And like the organization described above that was searching for a chief endowment officer, maybe we could differentiate between current and future or permanent impact—legacy impact officer or Office of Endowment Impact.

Steven Meyers, on the other hand, did not think this new title was a good one notwithstanding that he uses the word so frequently in his writing. He did acknowledge, however, that "donors do not know the many ways that the goal [personalized philanthropy] is frustrated by the very system we've created."[29] So in that case, he does agree with me. The system as it currently is structured in most places frequently just does not "work" for the donor but rather for the institution. However, this being said, in the long run, it may thwart the institution, too, because it may not be raising all that it could because of the way in which its fundraising is organized and marketed and the results of which are ultimately used as well as reported.

Do I expect that every philanthropic resource development office is going to change its name? Obviously not. Do I hope that these departments will focus more on the donor and the impact of gifts? Yes, of course. Do I wish that all donors and prospects receive attention across the board and not according to gift size or wealth screening? Absolutely, because I think that in the long run it is a much more respectful orientation to the contributor and silos between and among development offices will be reduced. Do I worry that less money will be raised for the not-for-profit sector as a result of these changes? Not at all, because if we prioritize "loyals" and baby boomers over the next few years, we shall raise a lot more money in that time than we might have without making change. Moreover, donors of smaller gifts might increase the size of their contributions if they feel that they have some meaning to or impact on the institutions that they support.

And while respect for the donor is key, there is more to this nomenclature issue than that. First, if we focus on retaining donors as opposed to the size of their respective gifts, there will be more individuals who will move to the "ultimate" gift category on the Donor Lifecycle Map no matter whether they are so-called major or not so major contributors. Second, I believe, like Simone Joyaux, that "vocabulary matters" especially in the world of fundraising.

She compares the words "philanthropy" and "fundraising," and she asks, "Which word generates hesitancy and maybe even suspicion? Which word produces smiles and gracious voice tones and positive words? Which word garners rather negative body language and less-than-positive words . . . and sometimes even distaste?"[30] The Office of Philanthropic Impact or even Philanthropic Resource Development could generate a much more positive reaction, I think, than so many of the labels we now use.

Joyaux goes on to describe her feelings toward other words in the fundraising vocabulary. She writes that she really "hates the term—'major.' Because," she explains, "if there is a major donor or major gift or major gift officer . . . that immediately suggests that there are minor gifts and minor donors and minor gift officers. And 'major' and 'minor' refer to gift size. That is so very, very offensive." Her comparison to Bill and Melinda Gates vividly demonstrates her point.

"Major gift donors Bill and Melinda—and your local Bill and Melinda—give major gifts. And somehow that makes them more special and more important. More special and important than Bob and Ben, married with three children, who've been giving $100 a year for a decade. Or Sarah and Sam, donors of $50 a year for twenty years. What an insult. How demeaning. And how very, very stupid."[31] There is no way that any of us cannot agree with her, but in the field of fund development, we behave just as she describes.

I would imagine, although I do not know, that she would "hate" the terms "planned and major gift officer" or even "Planned Giving Department."

These words just don't mean anything to the person wishing to make an endowment contribution.

Joyaux goes on to quote from a book that she wrote with Tom Ahern, *Keep Your Donors: The Guide to Better Communications and Stronger Relationships*. She writes,

> Philanthropy means voluntary action for the common good. Fund development is the essential partner of philanthropy. Fund development makes philanthropy possible by bringing together a particular cause, and donors and prospects who are willing to invest in the cause. The goal is to acquire donors of time and money who stay with the charity. This is done through the process of relationship building. With the donor at the center, fund development nurtures loyalty and lifetime value, thus facilitating philanthropy. You know if your relationship building works because your retention rates rise and the lifetime value of your donors and volunteers increases. [32]

So yes, language matters. Titles matter. Joyaux concludes, "And we fund-raisers can control the vocabulary. We workers in the nonprofit sector can pursue the right vocabulary to send the best messages for the greatest respect and care."[33]

And that's why I would like to change our language in relation to the departments in which we try to raise funds and, of course, especially the terms we use in reference to endowment development. I would like to focus on the concepts of philanthropy and the impact of contributions and especially bring clarity to the activity of endowment building.

NOTES

1. Mark Jones, interview with author, January 22, 2020, and follow-up e-mail, February 3, 2020.
2. Mark Jones, e-mail to author, February 3, 2020.
3. "Do You Have a Chief Legacy Officer?" Family Wealth Coach, September 16, 2013, https://www.familywealthcoach.com/2013/09/16/chief-legacy-officer/.
4. https://www.merriam-webster.com/dictionary/legacy.
5. Brian Sagrestano and Robert E. Wahlers, *Getting Started in Charitable Gift Planning: Your Guide to Planned Giving* (Nashville: Charity Channel Press, 2016), 9.
6. David J. Chused, interview with author, October 16, 2019, and subsequent e-mail to author, April 24, 2020.
7. https://www.indeed.com/q-director-of-gift-planning-jobs.html?vjk=e2cfdce73e47391d. Moreover, when I looked on the job sites of Indeed.com and *The Chronicle of Philanthropy* for the title, Chief Legacy Officer, a lot of "chiefs" surfaced but none with this particular designation.
8. https://www.joelpaul.com/fundraising/director-of-planned-giving-and-estates-ny-758/.
9. Doug White, e-mail to author, March 18, 2020.
10. The Fund Raising School, Lilly Family School of Philanthropy, "Planned Giving: Getting the Proper Start," 277.
11. The Fund Raising School, "Planned Giving," 208.
12. The Fund Raising School, "Planned Giving," 203–205.
13. https://www.shalomdc.org/endowment/.

14. Vandita Wilson, "University Donations Are Noble but in Need of Scrutiny," *The Justice*, September 24, 2019, 12.

15. Debra E. Blum, "Personalized Philanthropy: Group's Customized Giving Plans Show Big Results," *The Chronicle of Philanthropy*, April 4, 2016, https://www.weizmann-usa.org/media/2048/groups-customized-giving-plans-show-big-results-the-chronicle-of-philanthropy.pdf.

16. Blum, "Personalized Philanthropy."

17. Stacy B. Sulman, J.D., telephone conversation with author, January 31, 2020.

18. Stacy B. Sulman, J.D., telephone conversation with author, January 31, 2020.

19. Stacy B. Sulman, J.D., telephone conversation with author, January 31, 2020.

20. Blum, "Personalized Philanthropy."

21. Heather Joslyn, "It's Almost a Requirement Now to Tell Donors the Impact of Their Gifts," *The Chronicle of Philanthropy*, April, 2019, 14.

22. Wilson, "University Donations."

23. St. Jude Children's Research Hospital, "St. Jude Proton Therapy," brochure.

24. Steven L. Meyers, *Personalized Philanthropy: Crash the Fundraising Matrix* (Nashville: CharityChannel Press, 2015) 15.

25. Meyers, *Personalized Philanthropy*, 9.

26. Meyers, *Personalized Philanthropy*, 48.

27. David Chused, interview with author, October 16, 2019.

28. Stacy B. Sulman, telephone conversation with author, January 31, 2020.

29. Steven Meyers, e-mail to author, February 3, 2020.

30. Simone P. Joyaux, "Fund Raising Vocabulary: Words I Hate," Charity Channel, https://charitychannel.com/fundraising-vocabulary-words-i-hate/?fl_builder&print=print.

31. Joyaux, "Fund Raising Vocabulary."

32. Joyaux, "Fund Raising Vocabulary."

33. Joyaux, "Fund Raising Vocabulary."

Chapter Seven

It's Not All About Bequests

Giving USA: The Annual Report on Philanthropy is published yearly by the Giving U.S.A. Foundation, and its findings are based on data collected by the Indiana University Lilly Family School of Philanthropy. As its title suggests, it reports on the amount contributed to not-for-profit organizations in the United States, and it does so by source: foundations, corporations, individuals, and bequests.

I have always asked myself two questions when looking at the findings: (1) Don't bequests come from individuals? (2) Why are they separated into a unique category of their own?

Another interesting fact always captures my attention: "Receipts from bequests in the not for profit sector in 2018 were 9% of the $427.1 billion contributed to charity"—more than from corporations—"and bequest contributions have exceeded $30 billion in the past four years."[1] Moreover, the percentage of total giving from bequests has grown approximately 2 percent over the years since 2012, when it constituted 7 percent of the total amount donated ($316.23 billion), to 2017, when it made up 9 percent of the total of $410.02 billion. In other words, monies from realized bequests increased not only in percentage of the whole but also in actual dollars.

There are also two questions that come to my mind from these data. The first is how were these bequests used by the recipient organizations. Were they deposited in a permanent endowment fund or board-restricted account, spent upon receipt to help defray annual expenses, or a combination of these options?

The second question is why not-for-profit organizations spend so much time and energy trying to secure donations from corporations and often expend so little energy on seeking bequests. This second inquiry becomes even more important after reading a new report from Marts & Lundy and the Lilly

Family School of Philanthropy, *The Philanthropy Outlook: 2020 & 2021*, where it is reported that "giving by bequests will see the largest increase in 2020" while "gifts made by corporations" are expected to be "more tepid."[2]

Bequests are important; there is no doubt about that. However, the purpose of this chapter, "It's Not All About Bequests," is to reply to that institution that inspired me to write this book in the first place and that I described in chapter 1. You remember—the one that was only interested in establishing a bequest program.

That organization could have easily pursued endowment gifts using other techniques, in addition to bequests, that are easy to understand, implement, and manage. Moreover, a bequest usually requires an attorney or some other professional to prepare the appropriate documents. The gifts that I suggest in this chapter really do not need any such involvement although a donor might certainly choose to review his or her intentions with an adviser. These gifting mechanisms include an outright contribution to an endowment, establishment of a charitable gift annuity, and lifetime distributions from an individual retirement account (IRA). Since all of these donations depend upon current assets, the fundraiser and the donor together craft the documents describing how the contribution will be used. In other words, these options provide easy to implement opportunities for establishing permanent endowment funds. I also discuss donor-advised funds (DAF) at the end of the chapter because they, too, need no professional adviser to draft documents. On the other hand, they are useful to a very small number of organizations, and I include them in order to distinguish how they are currently being used by for-profit institutions and how they were first developed as a tool for endowment building particularly by community foundations. I recommend that they should continue to be used for that purpose.

OUTRIGHT ENDOWMENT GIFTS

I am always surprised that when people talk about creating endowment funds, they immediately presume that the mechanisms for doing so have some kind of future characteristic and therefore the charity won't be able to use the monies until after the death of the donor and/or income beneficiaries. This may not be the assumption about some less common gift-giving techniques such as charitable lead trusts,[3] but for the most part this is the outlook of a majority of professionals and corresponds to the Sagrestano and Wahlers equation that I first described in chapter 2: Planned Gifts = Endowment = Mission.[4]

We hardly ever speak about outright endowment contributions notwithstanding that they, too, are "planned" and future-oriented in that their creation is to ensure long-term sustainability of the organization to which the funds are donated. Sometimes these donations are included in discussions of major gifts or capital campaigns, but rarely are they discussed in and of themselves as a gift-giving technique for the purpose of building the endowment while simultaneously meeting the objectives of a donor. In my opinion, an outright endowment contribution should be a starting point for any discussion with the prospective contributor. This is how the outright gift is presented in the materials distributed through the Harold Grinspoon Foundation Life & Legacy program: it receives parallel or equal billing to contributions from an estate or that provide income, such as charitable gift annuities or remainder trusts.

Some people want to make an outright donation in memory or in honor of an individual or in order to ensure ongoing recognition of a person's or family's name. Organizations often establish minimum gift amounts for such opportunities (e.g., $10,000 or $25,000), but the purpose for the donor is to establish a lasting tribute. While bequests are often the tool used to make these gifts, it certainly does not have to be the case, although Adrian Sargeant and his colleagues entitle a chapter in their book about fundraising "Bequest, In Memoriam, and Tribute Giving,"[5] which is then followed by a chapter titled "Planned Giving." (They apparently recognize them as separate subjects when in practice the latter encompasses the former.)

Professional fundraisers do talk about blended gifts with potential contributors where a portion of a donation is outright and used to establish a permanent endowment and then some complementary amount is donated through a bequest or another tool or technique and added to the initial gift. The issue here is that a percentage of the gift is paid while the donor is alive and it is all well planned. Sometimes these donations are used to name a building that is in the process of being constructed or that is even completed. The notion is remembrance forever and usually by people that have had an ongoing connection with an institution.[6]

Outright endowment gifts can be restricted for a particular purpose as long as it is a broad one that will hopefully not become obsolete over time. Examples include funds for women and girls, scholarships, staff development or conference support, as well as services for children with special needs. Lectures and performances are often established to honor or memorialize individuals using outright endowment contributions. What's important is that a contingent use or some other language should always be included in the document establishing the fund just in case the original purpose becomes unnecessary, impossible to implement, or just generally not practical over time.

An outright endowment gift is particularly attractive because it provides the donor with the opportunity not only to express personal values but also to actually experience the joy of making the gift and seeing its impact while he or she is still alive. As a matter of fact, fundraisers who automatically suggest a bequest as opposed to discussing an outright endowment option with a donor often do the latter a disservice because it deprives the individual from enjoying the gift-making and/or results of it during his or her lifetime. Of course, current rules in some organizations about minimum gift size for establishing named endowment funds can quash a discussion, although smaller outright gifts could be pooled with larger ones or placed into an unrestricted fund and a donor's name included on a list of contributors or recognized in some other fashion.

Endowment giving is not all one way—for the benefit of the institution. (Remember that inappropriate name—"Office of Institutional Advancement"?) As noted by Weinstein and Barden, "Endowment funds are important to the nonprofit organization's long-term viability and financial health."[7] Of course they help the recipient organization. However, the donor is also a principal beneficiary, and Weinstein and Barden agree: "Contributions to endowment funds allow donors to make major investments in an organization and enable them to perpetuate their values."[8] An outright gift provides donors with the opportunity to see their named fund established, to observe the impact of their contribution, and to enjoy both the recognition and satisfaction that result. This may be the reason that so many not-for-profit organizations tell the story of living donors and the gifts they make in their marketing materials. Sure, the point of these pieces is to describe actual gifts and pique prospect curiosity and interest in doing something similar. But these stories also provide the contributors with recognition that those who agree to the publicity obviously enjoy. Moreover, they are also another "tool" for keeping the donor engaged. Someone has to interview the contributors, and the latter can obtain numerous copies of any publication to distribute to friends, relatives, and colleagues. In other words, the relationship between the donor and the institution keeps on growing stronger through interaction around the gift and its narrative.

CHARITABLE GIFT ANNUITIES (CGA)

When I began in the field of endowment development, I knew nothing about charitable gift annuities, even the simple ones that paid out an immediate income stream. After working on several of these, however, I recognized how easy they are to establish and manage. I also learned how attractive they could be to members of a baby boomer generation who had large amounts invested in the stock market. These gifts provide the donor with an opportunity to contribute highly appreciated stock, which is liquidated by the charity in order to establish the annuity. The contribution allows the donor to support an organization, retain an income stream, and obtain a tax deduction. It really is the proverbial "win-win" situation.[9]

There are many explanations as to how a charitable gift annuity operates. I have taken this one from *Getting Started in Charitable Gift Planning: The Resource Book*, which describes a charitable gift annuity as "a simple contract between the donor and a charity":

> In exchange for the irrevocable gift of cash, securities or other assets, the charity agrees to pay one or two annuitants (if a second is named) a fixed sum each year for life. The payments are secured by the general resources of the charity.
> The older the annuitants are at the time of the gift, the greater the fixed payment will be that is paid to the donor by the charity. In most cases, part of each payment is tax free, which increases each payment's after-tax value. [10]

Charities that issue charitable gift annuities customarily use payout rates that are recommended by the American Council on Gift Annuities and are based on an assumption that there will be a "50 percent residuum" remaining in the contract on the death of the income beneficiary or beneficiaries. [11] This is the amount that is intended to be ultimately available for the not-for-profit organization. The council also provides information about regulation requirements for creating a charitable gift annuity program. These vary from state to state. [12] "The issuing charity must also provide payment beneficiaries with form 1099-R, indicating how much was distributed [to each individual] and the taxation of payments." [13] There are multiple software programs that will calculate payout rates and taxation schedules related to the annuity.

The American Council on Gift Annuities website describes the characteristics of an individual who would be most interested in establishing a charitable gift annuity. A likely prospective donor is someone who is "retired" and wants "to increase [their] cash flow, seek the security of fixed payments that will not vary, and would like to save taxes." [14]

Sagrestano and Wahlers claim that charitable gift annuities are useful for the donor who wants to increase "income in retirement while also supporting a cause important" [15] to him or her. *The Philanthropy Outlook: 2020 & 2021* reinforces their statement: increases in giving will be related, among other factors, to "year-over-year growth in the current year's S&P 500" especially in relation to "those with median and higher levels of income." [16] (While this paragraph was written before the steep decline in market value in 2020 due to the coronavirus pandemic, hopefully it will return to former heights as occurred in other such situations and charitable gift annuities will retain their luster. On the other hand, these same tools might become more attractive to donors who want to not only increase their income stream but also obtain certainty in doing so by obtaining a fixed return while supporting their favorite charities.)

Some baby boomers hold shares in companies that have increased in value over the years, and many of these pay little or no dividend, such as

Facebook or Alphabet (Google). At the same time, individuals who hold these assets and would like to liquidate them in order to obtain their cash value cannot do so without paying capital gains tax on appreciation and thus reducing the amount that they will receive and have available to spend. This is not a very appealing option for some potential donors, and a charitable gift annuity could be attractive to them. (There are different kinds of charitable gift annuities, but I am referring to the easiest to establish as well as the most common.)

While most colleges, universities, and other large not-for-profit organizations issue charitable gift annuities, they could be a problem for a mid-size or smaller charity. This is because the legal requirements for establishing a program may serve as an obstacle for these institutions. At the same time, donors might not have confidence that the organization can maintain the required payments. But there are solutions to these challenges.

Let's start with the contract that legally requires the charity to pay the annuitant(s). If for some reason a charity finds that it cannot do so, it is still responsible for these payments. As a result of this obligation, many boards of directors of nonprofit organizations choose not to establish charitable gift annuity programs. They fear that over time they may not have the money that they would need to pay beneficiaries because of any number of reasons but particularly shortfalls in earnings or unwillingness to use organizational assets to fund required payments. On the other hand, the organization that I referred to in chapter 1 could easily have created a charitable gift annuity program. Its long history along with numerous properties could have provided the wherewithal to ensure that the payout was always met even if a building had to be sold or mortgaged. It also had the back office capacity to issue payments as well as prepare the required tax documents.

In comparison, however, I did work for an institution whose finances were precarious and whose board did not want to assume annuity contracts for fear that it might not be able to meet the payout obligations over the long term. However, its donor pool came from the entire state and beyond, and it had a robust annual giving program. There was also a well-established back room that could have handled the obligations associated with issuing gift annuities. In other words, there was an audience for a charitable gift annuity program and the internal capacity to manage one, but there was a valid fear about assuming the payout commitments.

An option for this organization was the community foundation that was willing to accept the responsibility for issuing charitable gift annuities on the institution's behalf and did so for several other local charities. There was a "hitch," however, from the perspective of the organization in question. The foundation required, since it was taking on the obligation of meeting the charitable gift annuity contracts, that once the income beneficiary or beneficiaries passed away, the residuum would remain in its permanent endowment as a restricted fund for the benefit of the organization. In other words, over time the latter would profit from an endowment fund notwithstanding that it would have no control over the investment and management of it. The community foundation would administer the endowment on the institution's behalf and provide the latter with an annual payout in accordance with the foundation's spending policy. It would charge a fee for the service, but this would be in line with foundation norms, and even if the charity were to manage its own endowment, it, too, would pay investment costs.

The community foundation option was a nice solution particularly in relation to two issues: the institution would have a pathway to start building a permanent endowment where none existed, and it could provide its donors with a mechanism to contribute and receive secure income over their respective lifetimes. The board, however, voted against working with the community foundation because it wanted access to the principal in tough times and the foundation by-laws did not allow that to happen.

In comparison, I consulted with a small cultural organization that had a donor population of older people and whose board recognized the need to launch an endowment program. This group immediately partnered with the community foundation in order to offer charitable gift annuities to its supporters while also simultaneously beginning to build the endowment by focusing on outright gifts as well as bequests.

The advantage of a charitable gift annuity program is that the organization that writes the contract can clearly include in it that the amount remaining in the annuity (the residuum), both income and principal, once the beneficiary is no longer alive, will be deposited into the permanent endowment and used according to any restrictions imposed (or lack thereof) by the donor. As a matter of fact, this directive should be included in the guidelines of all such programs and should appear on templates of annuity contracts so that the donor knows from the "get-go" that this is the modus operandi of the charity. The contract could also include any ultimate name that the endowment fund might bear if such an opportunity is made available by the institution.

The United States Holocaust Memorial Museum provides a clear example of this kind of directive and it appears on its website where model language is posted: "Upon termination of the charitable gift annuity, the remaining principal will be used to support the Museum's Permanent Endowment Fund or another specified purpose you may have designated."[17] In comparison, some other charities recommend the same language for their annuity program as they do for a bequest: the remaining funds, after the demise of the income beneficiary, will be used "for the general purposes of the organization." The concept of the permanent endowment is not specifically stated in these cases nor is the final depository of the funds even mentioned. I wonder if these issues are even discussed with donors when contracts are written.

OUTRIGHT DISTRIBUTION FROM A RETIREMENT FUND

An outright distribution from a retirement account provides another opportunity for a donor to establish a permanent endowment fund while alive. The professional fundraiser and the contributor together draft the document creating the fund, and as a result there is no ambiguity about how the donation will be used and where it will be deposited.

Not-for-profit organizations have come to realize, especially in the current tax environment when it is increasingly difficult to itemize charitable contributions, that an outright distribution from a retirement fund can be a very powerful gift both for the institution and the donor. The rule is easy: "If you are 70 1/2 or older, you can transfer up to $100,000 to charity tax-free each year—even if that's more than your RMD [required minimum distribution]. The money counts as your required minimum distribution but isn't included in your adjusted gross income."[18] In other words, individuals who make these donations pay no income tax on the distribution and they also receive no tax deduction. The law only applies to distributions from an IRA, not a 401(k) or other kind of retirement account, although the latter can be transferred to a traditional IRA and the gift ultimately made.[19] As noted in chapter 5, there have been changes to the law in 2020 due to the coronavirus pandemic, and a *Wall Street Journal* article advises that "wealthy donors who want to give more than $100,000 of IRA assets also have a new way to do it this year only, due to a provision in the newly passed Cares Act stimulus legislation." The most important part of the article is the instruction "to learn more, consult a tax advisor."[20]

I did not quite understand the power of the law relating to RMD distributions until I listened to a donor relate how he had used it to benefit two not-for-profit organizations that he had supported over time and about which he cared deeply. I described this situation in chapter 5, "Who Are Endowment Donors?" He was a wealthy individual and explained that not only did he not need the money from his IRA but he certainly did not want to pay income tax on it and so, if you remember, over the course of ten years he transferred $100,000 a year from his IRA to two charities and thus over that timespan had built up a $500,000 endowment fund at each. What a powerful contribution. This gentleman clearly enjoyed making these donations as well as discussing them publicly.

I have read so many articles in not-for-profit publications that tell similar stories to the one described above. For example, in a Massachusetts Institute of Technology (MIT) "gift planning" brochure, there is a description of a woman who wanted to memorialize her husband and thus decided to set up a scholarship in his name using what she supposed would be eventual "funding" from her IRA after death. However, when the tax laws changed, she explained, "I was advised that using qualified charitable IRA distributions would be a beneficial way to contribute as it kept my adjusted gross income down and allowed me to meet minimum distribution requirements."[21] She, too, was reportedly thrilled with the gift and especially its impact on undergraduates. Her story concludes: "Giving a scholarship to MIT will help students, but this process has also enriched my life as a donor in ways that could not be anticipated."[22]

Increasing numbers of charitable organizations recognize that a large portion of their "loyal" donor population is ripe for these contributions, whether individuals leaving the job market with retirement assets to distribute or baby boomers who have reached the age when they must withdraw their required minimum distribution but continue to work. Some of these people neither need the funds nor want to pay taxes on them, and they are particularly good candidates for outright gifts of their RMDs or a portion of them to charity. While $100,000 is the limit that is allowed for distributions to nonprofit organizations from an IRA with no tax liability, gifts can be of any size. The important fact is that the contribution is outright and can be used to establish a named endowment fund. Moreover, if the charity allows, the donor can also direct how the latter will be used.

There are multiple reasons that I have described these examples of both outright and income-producing contributions. First and most important is that there is no question as to the ultimate repository of the donations; they can be used to establish permanent endowment funds while the donor is alive. Second, the age group for these gifts is particularly fitting to baby boomers who have acquired significant assets over time. And the third is the personal satisfaction that the gift giving provides to the donor—a fact that we cannot forget in the charitable world of "institutional advancement." And while I have concentrated here on the outright gift of retirement assets, and while this is not a book describing all of the various ways that someone can make a future contribution to charity, I don't want any reader to think that I am neglecting the fact that a donor can instruct that retirement assets be distributed to one or more not-for-profit organizations after the death of the account holder. This is a very powerful gift, too, but unless the supporter states very clearly that his or her contribution is to be used to establish a permanent endowment fund, it might not happen. An outright gift while alive ensures that ultimate purpose.

DONOR-ADVISED FUNDS (DAF)

I cannot write a book on endowment building without mentioning the role or lack thereof of donor-advised funds in the enterprise. I use the latter word cogently because these funds have become commercial in their evolution and, I think, have lost their raison d'etre in so many instances. As noted at the beginning of this chapter, I have included them here because no professional adviser is needed to draft the documents establishing these funds; agreements are simple to execute and increasingly are completed using the Internet. Donor-advised funds are not a common mechanism for endowment building among most not-for-profit organizations because the administration of them is demanding in terms of reporting and accounting, and therefore, they are usually only offered by those institutions that have a well-functioning back room.

Donor-advised funds are donative tools that were originally adopted by community foundations as a mechanism that would eventually lead to endowment building. That was their ultimate purpose.

The first donor-advised funds were established in 1931 by the New York Community Trust and became popular in 1969 because of the Tax Reform Act of that year. DAFs are named by the donor and pooled for investment purposes; their particularly unique feature is that contributors can "recommend" not-for-profit organizations to receive grants from their personalized funds. Donors suggest these allocations as opposed to making them outright because they do not "own" the funds. The not-for-profit organization that "houses" the donor-advised fund and from which the contributor receives a tax deduction for establishing it is in fact the owner. Donor-advised funds are often described as inexpensive alternatives to a private foundation.

The Council on Foundations describes a donor-advised fund in the following way: "A donor advised fund (DAF) is a type of charitable giving fund that is established by a donor with an eligible charitable sponsoring organization (i.e. a community foundation) to support a cause (or causes) that the donor cares about. A donor advised fund allows the donor to remain involved and active in charitable giving by retaining 'advisory privileges' to recommend how the sponsoring organization should make grants from that fund."[23]

As far as donors are concerned, they "relinquish all ownership and control over the donated funds or property," and while they can make recommendations as to distributions from their named funds, the charitable organization that owns the funds is "free to accept or reject any suggestion or request made by a donor."[24] Most sponsoring organizations rarely reject donor recommendations for fear of antagonizing contributors and losing "business."

So if donor-advised funds are only attractive to the largest and most administratively competent organizations, you might ask why I am including them in a book about endowment development. My answer is that when they were first introduced, they were viewed as a conduit or a tool for building permanent endowment funds especially in community foundations. Because of this purpose, a minimum amount, whether cash, appreciated stock, or another asset, was necessary to start a fund—anywhere from $2,500 to $10,000—in order to make them accessible to "middle-class and middle-class affluent" donors. If this base sum was not maintained, the remaining balance could be "swept" into the permanent endowment, sometimes maintaining the fund name and sometimes not. In addition, a limited number of so-called recommenders could be assigned to the fund (usually one generation after the founder) so that at the end of the last individual's lifetime, the remaining balance would be placed into the permanent endowment. One of the purposes of these funds was to introduce donors to the organization that housed them, and hopefully, as a result of establishing stronger connections, these contributors would create permanent endowment funds either through the transfer of the DAF, the establishment of another fund such as one designated for a purpose or local organization, or a combination thereof. In other words, donor-advised funds were viewed as mechanisms to encourage contributors to become more involved with the not-for-profit so that they might ultimately establish a permanent endowment fund therein.

It appears that the San Diego Foundation (and probably others, too) still envisions this purpose for donor-advised funds. It is written on its website: "Some donors maintain both an endowment fund and a non-endowment fund, allowing them to regularly transfer monies from the non-endowment fund to the endowment fund to help build a balance upon which gifts can be provided in perpetuity."[25] The non-endowment fund in this case is the donor-advised fund, and what is interesting is that the foundation not only distinguishes between the two types of funds but states that "an advised non-endowment fund can become an endowment fund at any time upon request."[26]

The Community Foundation for Greater New Haven in Connecticut is another example of a foundation that promotes the ultimate depository of donor-advised funds as the permanent endowment. Its website explains that there is an option among differing models of donor-advised funds of the "Perpetual Fund," which "seeks to preserve the real economic spending power of your donor advised fund over time. To meet this objective, only a percentage (%) of your fund's market value is available to recommend for grantmaking each year."[27]

Donor-advised funds seem to me to have somehow lost their function as tools for endowment building because of the onslaught of commercial funds and even those offered by some not-for-profit organizations with high thresholds ($100,000 to $1 million). In addition, in the latter set of organizations, they have become a vehicle solely for the "major donor," which is fine but ignores that somewhat affluent baby boomer generation that will be shortly passing on its wealth.

My issue is not with the large not-for-profit organizations that have established donor-advised funds as giving vehicles because, for the most part, they have done so to increase the amount that the fund holders donate to the organization that is in fact managing them. This is a tool for them to increase contributions—primarily annual—from their wealthiest supporters. So for example, at the Massachusetts Institute of Technology, while $1 million is the minimum gift to establish such a fund, at least 50 percent of it must be designated for "MIT purposes."[28] Moreover, this donor-advised fund is marketed as "a sustaining gift for MIT's future," and so I assume that because it is "sustaining" that ultimately whatever is left in the fund at the demise of the recommender(s) will be placed in the permanent endowment fund. Another example of a large not-for-profit organization that maintains a donor-advised fund program is the Nature Conservancy, which requires a $100,000 minimum gift to establish a fund and at least 20 percent of it must be allocated to that organization.[29]

The issue here is that these funds that were originally designed for the purpose of creating a permanent endowment over time have turned into a commercial vehicle with no endowment-building features. Moreover, they have come to dominate the market for donor-advised funds, often taking "customers" from the not-for-profit sector and especially from community foundations. They have become so attractive that Fidelity's Charitable Gift Fund was ranked "No 1" in the 2016 "Philanthropy 400" and has retained that position ever since.[30] And a 2019 article in *The Chronicle of Philanthropy* reports that "Fidelity Charitable took in $9 billion last year, triple the $3.0 billion United Way Worldwide raised. In fact, the donor-advised fund giant brought in more contributions in 2018 than the top five nonprofits on the America's Favorite Charities list combined. Donations to the top five DAFs grew more than 28 percent last year."[31]

The problem is that these commercial competitors have no permanent endowment characteristics whatsoever notwithstanding that both Vanguard and Fidelity now offer end-of-fund-life alternatives through what they call "Legacy Planning"[32] and the "Endowed Giving Program,"[33] respectively. Neither of these resembles a permanent endowment in a not-for-profit organization unless the donor deliberately inserts a recommendation that remaining sums in the fund be distributed to a charity for such a purpose. When a fund is established online, this kind of thinking is not often present or even considered.

There have been many articles over time that critique these commercial funds for any number of reasons. I am not going to summarize the arguments for or against except where they coincide with my own concerns. First, most organizations that offer donor-advised funds, whether not-for-profit or commercial, charge fees—sometimes for administering the fund, a separate sum for investing assets, or a combination of both—but in the for-profit sector these fees go "to the bottom line." In other words, commercial entities offer these funds because they are a source of profit. There is no charitable purpose whatsoever. In comparison, in the not-for-profit sector, donor-advised funds are usually invested with the permanent endowment; fees defray costs and ensure that an ever increasing amount of the unrestricted endowment reaches the population served by the organization. It does not matter if the organization is a community foundation, an educational institution, or other charitable entity.

There were many individuals who commented on the first *Chronicle of Philanthropy* article cited above, "Fidelity Charitable Pushes United Way Out of Top Place." One respondent claimed that all of the for-profit funds, including "Fidelity, Schwab, and other commercially based DAFs make money when their donors *DON'T* give from their giving accounts" (emphasis in the original), which was an interesting comment since it is true that fees will increase the more money that remains in the fund. There were other people who expressed concern over the close link of donor-advised funds to the "financial service industry," and one just referred to them as an indicator of "a money management mindset."[34]

Robert Sharpe, however, a well-known expert in the field of not-for-profit endowment development, added to the comments, and he supported the development of commercial donor advised funds. However, he made an interesting comparison. He wrote, "The community foundation as the true owner of the funds would step in and transfer them to an unrestricted community endowment or directly to one or more charities in the discretion of the board of the community foundation." He compared this behavior with that of the for-profit entities that do no such thing. In other words, Sharpe recognized that in the short run the funds offered by the for-profit and not-for-profit sectors, and especially those offered by community foundations, were more or less alike. However, in the long run they were administered very differently since those that operated in the not-for-profit arena and especially by community foundations were intended over time to become permanent endowments that would have impact on local populations, which was certainly not the case for the commercial entities.[35]

In order to attract contributors and to compete more effectively with money-making donor-advised funds, some community foundations are reducing the size of their required minimum gift size and increasing the number of generations that can serve as "recommenders." In other words, they are "lowering the bar" for entering into a donor-advised fund relationship with a contributor, and by doing so, they are also weakening their attention to mission.

This issue became very clear to me when I met with a chief executive officer of a community foundation. He described to me how he had "lost" three donor-advised funds because of the requirement that a certain amount—in this case $10,000—could never be "recommended" out but rather had to remain as a permanent endowment fund within the foundation. He told me that the millennial generation that was tied to electronics viewed the DAF as an Internet-based, philanthropic checkbook and that their interest was making a tax-deductible gift and then spending it over time. He explained that he was considering a recommendation to his board that would change the rules for donor-advised funds so that his organization might compete more effectively with those for-profit operations that had a lower required minimum to open and maintain a DAF.

We talked about the mission of his organization: to establish a permanent endowment to ensure that future generations have access to the same or even higher-quality services than those currently available in the community. He was unsure that this was a compelling enough rationale for millennials at this stage in their lives. I argued for not forgetting the raison d'etre of the institution.

I am not sure how he resolved the issue, but the conversation addresses the difference between an organization whose purpose is to build a permanent endowment for the benefit of a community and a commercial "checking account." It also points to the fact that the younger generation may not have yet had the time to build up loyalty to an organization and therefore have any vision for its future and their role in securing it.

Welcome the baby boomers!

NOTES

1. https://givingusa.org/just-released-special-report-leaving-a-legacy-a-new-look-at-planned-giving-donors/.

2. Marts & Lundy and Lilly Family School of Philanthropy, *The Philanthropy Outlook: 2020 & 2021*, February 2020, 2.

3. A charitable lead trust is an irrevocable trust designed to provide financial support to one or more charities for a period of time, with the remaining assets eventually going to family members or other beneficiaries. Charitable lead trusts are often considered to be the inverse of a *charitable remainder trust.* https://www.fidelitycharitable.org/guidance/philanthropy/charitable-lead-trusts.html.

4. Brian Sagrestano and Robert E. Wahlers, *Getting Started in Charitable Gift Planning: Your Guide to Planned Giving* (Nashville: Charity Channel Press, 2016), 17.

5. Adrian Sargeant, Jen Shang, and Associates, *Fundraising Principles and Practice*, 2nd ed. (Hoboken: John Wiley and Sons, 2017), 463.

6. I once had donors who were incredibly committed to an organization and especially the history of the medium that it celebrated. A library was already built on the campus, but this couple wanted it named after them and established a permanent endowment through an outright gift to be paid over five years specifying that the building would bear their name. This same behavior occurred with another institution for which I worked. These naming opportunities were attached to portions of an organization's physical complex that were already built, and notwithstanding that fact, they were attractive to select donors.

7. Stanley Weinstein and Pamela Barden, *The Complete Guide to Fundraising Management*, 4th ed. (Hoboken, NJ: John Wiley and Sons, 2017), 219.

8. Weinstein and Barden, *The Complete Guide*, 219.

9. I did have a few donors who established charitable gift annuities using cash but they were fewer than those using appreciated stock.

10. Brian M. Sagrestano and Robert E. Wahlers, *Getting Started in Charitable Gift Planning: The Resource Book*, 13–14.

11. Sagrestano and Wahlers, *Getting Started*, 16.

12. See http://acga-web.org.

13. Sagrestano and Wahlers, *Getting Started*, 19.

14. https://www.acga-web.org/public-resources/donor-information.

15. Sagrestano and Wahlers, *Getting Started*, 14.

16. Marts & Lundy and Lilly Family School of Philanthropy, *The Philanthropy Outlook*, 4. This paragraph was written before the current depreciation of the equity market due to the coronavirus scare.

17. https://www.ushmm.org/support/ways-to-give/planned-giving/options#Deferred%20Charitable%20Gift%20Annuity.

18. "FAQs About Giving Your RMD to Charity," Kiplinger, Washington, D.C., https://www.kiplinger.com/article/retirement/T045-C001-S003-faqs-about-giving-your-rmd-to-charity.html.

19. "FAQs About Giving Your RMD to Charity."

20. Laura Saunders, "It's Time for a New Approach to Charitable Donations," *The Wall Street Journal*, April 18–19, 2020, B5.

21. Massachusetts Institute of Technology, "A World of Difference," *Corridor*, Fall 2018.

22. Massachusetts Institute of Technology, "A World."

23. https://www.cof.org/public-policy/donor-advised-funds.

24. Council on Foundations, *Donor Advised Fund Timeline*, https://www.cof.org/sites/default/files/documents/files/DAF-timeline.pdf.

25. https://www.sdfoundation.org/news-events/sdf-news/endowment-funds-vs-nonendowment-funds-whats-difference/.

26. https://www.sdfoundation.org/news-events/sdf-news/endowment-funds-vs-nonendowment-funds-whats-difference.

27. https://www.cfgnh.org/increasing-giving/charitable-fund-options/what-is-a-donor-advised-fund/how-dafs-work.

28. Massachusetts Institute of Technology, "MIT Donor-Advised Fund. A sustaining gift for MIT's future."

29. https://www.nature.org/en-us/membership-and-giving/donate-to-our-mission/gift-and-estate-planning/all-planned-giving-options/donor-advised-funds/?tab_q=tab_container-tab_element.

30. Drew Lindsay, Peter Olsen-Phillips, and Eden Stiffman, "Fidelity Charitable Pushes United Way Out of Top Place in Ranking of the 400 U.S. Charities That Raise the Most," *The Chronicle of Philanthropy*, October 27, 2016, https://www.philanthropy.com/article/Fidelity-Charitable-Knocks/238167.

31. Eden Stiffman and Emily Haynes, "Anxiety in Times of Plenty," *The Chronicle of Philanthropy*, November 5, 2019, https://www.philanthropy.com/interactives/20191105-Favorite-Charities-2019.

32. https://www.vanguardcharitable.org/giving-with-vc/how-it-works/legacy-planning.

33. https://www.fidelitycharitable.org/content/dam/fc-public/docs/programs/fidelity-charitable-program-guidelines.pdf, 22–27.

34. Lindsay, Olsen-Phillips, and Stiffman, "Fidelity Charitable Pushes United Way."

35. Lindsay, Olsen-Phillips, and Stiffman, "Fidelity Charitable Pushes United Way."

Chapter Eight

How to Build an Endowment Program

If you have reached this point, you expect that this chapter is for beginners—those people who are considering the establishment of an endowment program but have not done so. If you are an experienced endowment development professional or board member, you think you have nothing more to read. But, whoever you are, please continue because the most important part of building an endowment is the policies established to ensure its growth. These are critical to everyone in the field and dependent upon the vision of the executive staff along with the board of an institution. I shall discuss the roles of these individuals in this chapter, among other topics, and therefore no matter how large your organization's endowment currently is or how long it has been in existence, there are significant items for you notwithstanding your level of experience. For example, if there are no specific or even consistent policies about the use of unrestricted bequests, this chapter is for you. Or, if your organization is bemoaning the size and therefore the limitations of its endowment purchasing power, please keep reading.

Writers in the field often create inventories of requirements that must be in place before any effort to build an endowment fund is pursued. In my opinion, there is only one such prerequisite—prospects—especially those that have been donating ten to fifteen years, and if they are baby boomers, all the better.[1] So if the latter are among your longtime donors, then it is time to immediately get started, and for those organizations that have programs, it is time to focus on this population group. That is not to say that younger people should be ignored; it is to say that baby boomers need a concentrated effort or, better yet, strategy.

Notwithstanding that so many organizations link their endowment development and major gift programs, there is no proof that I have come across that the two are related. "The idea that planned giving donors are always major donors during their lifetime is a myth," reports Eden Stiffman in *The Chronicle of Philanthropy*.[2] And another article in *The Chronicle* describes the endeavor of the Nature Conservancy that is "ratcheting up efforts to reach out to its most loyal donors in a more personalized fashion." Size of gift is never mentioned as an important criterion in the organization's initiative— just loyalty. The rationale for the increased intensity, continues the article, was due in part to "looking at the baby boomers, looking at the demographics" where the charity counted "about 370,000 donors who are boomers." The article describes how "a pilot program in California, launched in 2016, which aims to raise pledged bequests from donors, had a response rate close to 6 percent—higher than other types of fundraising, such as direct mail, which has a response rate of around 2 percent."[3]

So if there are prospects, it's time to get started. As Stanley Weinstein and Pamela Barden write in their book, *The Complete Guide to Fundraising Management*, "If you establish the endowment fund, people will donate. Donors rarely think of contributing to an endowment fund that has not been established. However, by establishing the fund and referring to it in public statements and in the organization's publications, the endowment seems to take on a life of its own." Then, not surprisingly, the chapter continues that the "simplest" and "most effective way to ensure healthy growth of the endowment is to publicize the bequests program."[4]

Once prospects are identified, there are items that must be put in place before launching an endowment development initiative. The three most important are policies for managing the program, a marketing strategy, and the assignment of responsibility for oversight. Of course, the support of the chief executive officer (CEO) and the board are essential. As a matter of fact, the vision of the chief executive is probably almost as important as potential donors.

The chief executive officer is the person who sets the tone for success in fundraising—all fundraising—by ensuring that there is a culture of philanthropy throughout an organization. He or she is the individual who must make certain that everyone is "on board" and who determines how an endowment program is implemented.

I have stated before in this book, especially in chapter 4, that leadership is an essential element of endowment building. I wrote in that chapter that one of the factors that make the Grinspoon Life & Legacy program so effective is the support of "senior staff and the board," and I quoted the director, Arlene Schiff, who unequivocally states that leadership is fundamental to the success of the program.[5] Therefore, since Life & Legacy is my model of what really "works" in endowment building, then that element is central to all such efforts.[6]

There are some basic aspects that increase the likelihood of success in endowment building, and most of them have to do with how resources are utilized within an organization as a whole and within the fundraising department in particular. This allocation is the responsibility of the chief executive officer. He or she proposes a budget that is eventually approved by a board. All of the elements that promote success, especially when silos between every type of fundraising are broken down, are determined by the vision of the CEO. He or she is the person who hires the primary philanthropic impact officer and dictates how the organization will move forward especially in relation to the culture of philanthropy where everyone within an institution is responsible for understanding fundraising and his or her role in relation to that function.

An article in *The Chronicle of Philanthropy* supports this perspective. The author writes, "When Kim Callinan was promoted to CEO of Compassion & Choices a year ago, she made many changes. One of them, she learned from fundraisers was unusual: She immediately directed more of the group's resources toward planned giving."[7] The critical word in this description is "unusual," and notwithstanding the planned giving verbiage, one of the goals of this book is to make this orientation "usual" with every CEO. The article continues, "Upon taking charge, Callinan also began to put in place plans to create a culture of philanthropy throughout the organization, making it clear that bringing in resources to further the mission was part of every employee's job."[8]

My own personal experience has confirmed for me that when the chief executive officer supports the endowment development effort and allows training of all staff members on their respective roles in fundraising and especially in identifying potential endowment contributors, then the initiative succeeds. In my case, when I was allotted time in staff meetings to describe the characteristics of endowment prospects as well as recent contributions that we received, fellow employees were interested and engaged in the conversation. I talked about the donor, how he or she came to our attention, and what kind of gift was closed. This system worked. Personnel from a variety of departments enthusiastically brought prospects to my attention, and all of these referrals resulted in endowment contributions. Only in one of my positions, where the CEO wanted no change from the current fundraising operation and where it became my responsibility alone to raise endowment monies, was the effort not very successful. There was so much potential in this organization given thousands of loyal donors but no leadership from the top.

In my positions with CEO support, board members were also trained about endowment giving and they, too, often made referrals. I was very lucky in the organizations in which I worked—all of them—because there was no question about the ultimate disposition of any realized future gift. They were all placed into the permanent endowment. The goal was always to increase its size through both contributions and investment.

The CEO, however, is not alone in articulating an endowment-building vision. It is crucial that board members support the lead of the CEO, or if the latter is not pursuing such a path, then they must make endowment development a priority, especially now where there is an impending as well as current transfer of wealth.

Board members must fully participate in the endowment-building process in a variety of ways. First, they need to ensure that there are by-laws in place that direct how endowment gifts will be treated—especially those that are unrestricted upon receipt. Second, they must provide a budget for the implementation of a program. Third, they must learn about endowment development including the characteristics of a prospective donor and the benefits to the latter of such contributions so that they might not only make referrals but also cogently speak about endowment giving to potential supporters. Fourth, they, too, like the CEO, must have a long-term vision and understand that fruition might take some time. Finally, since it is assumed that board members are supporters of the institutions where they serve, they must make provisions for their own endowment contributions. These are very substantial responsibilities.

Let's start with the first—approving an endowment-building program. So many writers on this subject caution readers that boards of directors might not want to support these initiatives. Scott C. Stevenson in his article, "How to Start an Endowment for Your Nonprofit," issues a "*Warning.*" He says that "small nonprofits may be criticized for not spending every dime on current needs. The organization's board of directors could be the biggest critics of an endowment." He continues, "Small and *new nonprofits* often only think about the current *fiscal year* or the next payroll. It is essential to get out of that financial trap as soon as possible. And endowment helps diversify your organization's income and reduces your vulnerability to every economic crisis"[9] (emphasis in the original). Stevenson assumes that even small organizations have "potential donors."[10]

Douglas White, an expert in the field, wrote about the role of boards in his 1995 book, *The Art of Planned Giving*. He noted that the role of "trustees" is essential to the success of a "planned giving program." He writes that trustees are an organization's "caretakers" and as such are "responsible for its present *and* its future" (emphasis in the original). He continues, "Too many trustees do not obligate themselves seriously enough to ensure a charity's future,"[11] and he describes the rationale for that viewpoint: "Despite many words to the contrary, the charity's trustees may not be ready to begin a planned giving program. Certainly a charity whose trustees are unwilling to see far into the future is almost defined as a charity unready to begin a planned giving program."[12] He blames some of this kind of decision-making on an organization's lack of prospects or "clarity of mission." But then he moves to a reason that is far more serious. He writes,

The big question here is one of commitment. Commitment requires patience and intelligent conviction.

A trustee who sits on the board solely because of his record of making current gifts may not understand or appreciate why a planned giving program is important, and a trustee who questions the need for planned giving is not yet ready to support a program that asks people for gifts that will not materialize for more than a decade or two. This attitude might be acceptable for organizations that do not care if they will exist in another generation, but for those who do, trustees need to know about planned giving.[13]

He then goes on to enumerate the responsibilities of board members, and they are very similar to the ones that I describe above. Trustees need to "generally know how the gifts work, what the advantages are to the donor, and their appeal. They must also understand that a good program does not blossom overnight." He also writes that "this is easy and obvious to assert, but far too many trustees have no idea how planned giving might fit into the overall development picture."[14]

While White seems to put the responsibility of not understanding onto the trustees themselves, it is an issue of education, and that is why I have always thought that the CEO plays the primary role in the process. He or she has the responsibility of teaching the board or finding someone to do so, whether it's a consultant, a staff member of a local community foundation, or some other expert, about the necessity of endowment building in safeguarding the organization for future generations. However, once this training has taken place—in no matter what form it occurs—if a board is still not prepared to move forward "at a healthy organization," then Doug White's words make sense: "The concern has evolved into an unhealthy paranoia that prevents a charity from forming an important financial lifeline to the future."[15] He asks the question, "Are Trustees Afraid of Planned Giving?" and continues, "Worrying about the payroll is easier and more defined than maintaining a long-range vision, so it is no wonder that planned giving is a difficult concept for trustees. That is no excuse, however, to delay."[16]

The alarming part of these comments is that he wrote them approximately twenty years ago and they still pertain today. Remember that seventy-year-old organization that inspired this book? Well, here is the e-mail that the director sent to me when I proposed an endowment development initiative: "The president and chairman and a few financial committee [members] all agreed that we definitely need to tackle planned giving." (I did not use that term in my initial inquiry; she did in her reply, however.) "At this time they feel they want me to focus on the [annual] dinner and the issues in the office. I hear them. We are a small team. The other issue is the cost."[17]

This organization is certainly not alone; I received a similar e-mail that I quoted in my first book. The institution had been in existence for thirty-five years, and its fundraising success was dependent on the charisma of its founder and leader, who was growing older. There was a huge reservoir of loyal donors, and there had been a short-lived endowment-building effort. The problem, however, was that the initiative was begun without any board input and thus support. The e-mail that I received stated, "The desire to move forward [with endowment building] is great; [however,] meeting the daily, weekly, and monthly needs has become all consuming. . . . All our efforts have been focused on obtaining [pledge] payments. At the same time, we are now behind in solicitations for next year."[18] Both of these e-mails reflect a board as well as CEO who can only envision current issues and are simultaneously without long-term vision.

In an article entitled "A Planned-Giving 'Nirvana,'" in *The Chronicle of Philanthropy*, the reporter describes how the board of trustees at the Nature Conservancy supported the endowment-building program, and she quotes an executive of the organization: "A lot of organizations cut back on planned-gift fundraising during tough economic times, preferring to focus on getting more dollars in the short term. 'The Nature Conservancy has never done that . . . There's been a commitment toward [planned giving], and that has paid off.'"[19] This reporter includes a sidebar within this article entitled "What the Wealth Transfer Means to Charities" and writes that the Nature Conservancy "with its sophisticated operation aimed at capturing planned gifts, is a step ahead of most charities in preparing for the historic transfer of wealth that's starting to happen—and the opportunities it presents for fund-raising."[20]

Once the CEO and the board of a not-for-profit organization have agreed to move forward with an endowment development program, there are several decisions that they must make. The most important issue is the necessity to create a vision statement or state a goal that communicates that the ultimate purpose of the endeavor is to build a permanent endowment. The second step is to pass a by-law that requires all future, unrestricted gifts to be deposited into the quasi-endowment and to include a mechanism that makes it difficult to access these assets for current spending. No outright spending upon receipt should be permitted notwithstanding, as I have noted, that any by-law can be changed. At least the discussion will occur and a consensus develop.

I described in chapter 7, "It's Not All About Bequests," the kinds of donations that are easy for organizations to encourage at the outset of an initiative—outright contributions, bequests, current IRA gifts taking advantage of the tax laws surrounding required minimum distributions, as well as charitable gift annuities whether under the organization's own auspice or that of a third party such as a community foundation. The CEO and board must agree on a budget that will include provisions for staffing the effort, training, and marketing. Other issues that need to be considered include money management, especially investment and spending policies. Decision makers must also decide when it is appropriate for an organization to serve as trustee of trusts and when not. Here again, there are consultants as well as community foundations that can provide assistance to an organization weighing all of these issues. And while there are other considerations, these are the basic ones that must be discussed and resolved before a formal endowment program is launched.

The question of whether and how to staff a new program can sometimes serve as an impediment to starting one. However, after so many years of working in endowment development, I have concluded that while a new hire is not necessary especially at the beginning of an initiative, someone must be assigned the task of ensuring that the program is organized and operating effectively; otherwise it will fail before it even begins. While there is a consensus in the field that everyone in the fundraising department and even beyond needs to serve as an endowment development officer and not only recognize gift opportunities and in many cases know how to close them, someone must be in charge.

Stiffman writes in her article, "Setting Up a Planned Giving Program," that it is preferable to "assign a point person on staff" who will "be the resource and the point of contact to answer any questions." She continues, "The era of the planned-giving expert and specialist on staff is passing. . . . Nonprofit fundraisers are asked to handle multiple types of donations—annual gifts, planned gifts, major gifts—all at the same time."[21] And Steve Meyers is correct when he describes development officers as "enlightened generalists," who will be "creative" and learn how to "balance both the compelling needs of donors and the compelling needs of our institutions."[22] This is certainly the ultimate goal in fund development and terrific where it is actually happening. However, there is a difference in being able to discuss and handle multiple gift types as well as donors and managing a program. The latter entails ensuring that policies are discussed and decided; the back office is operating; a marketing plan is developed, implemented, and altered over time; reports are made to the board; and everyone involved is constantly educated about the role and purpose of establishing an endowment program. It is then, of course, up to the chief executive officer in terms of how the position is staffed—whether part-time, full-time, or in place of another assignment that may in fact be obsolete or not necessary to the extent it once was. Remember that article described above about Kim Callinan and her "unusual" steps in changing the direction of her organization to put more "resources toward planned giving"? She began by revising "all of the staff's job descriptions" and introducing a "'double ask' protocol for fundraising."[23] And in the Nature Conservancy silos were broken down between "gift planning and major gifts."[24] In all of these cases, it took leadership to effect change, and that is what *The Chronicle of Philanthropy* author of both articles, Heather Joslyn, emphasizes in describing these cases.

In addition to the items that I have described as important for launching an endowment program—prospects, policies, leadership, and staffing—it is also essential to have a strategic plan not only for getting started but also for maintaining the initiative. Such a plan should include a timeline as well as steps for developing relationships with professional advisers; for providing ongoing training and education for an array of stakeholders including prospects, donors, staff, and board members; and for marketing. Guidelines and mechanisms for donor recognition must be constantly designed and refined as experience grows. I am not going to write in depth about all of these because there are so many resources in the field, but I shall make a few comments about areas that I think are not only important but often overlooked by not-for-profit organizations getting started in or operating an endowment development program.

POLICIES FOR ESTABLISHING AND
MARKETING ENDOWMENT FUNDS

The policies for establishing and marketing endowment funds particularly in relation to minimum gift levels have an impact on the growth of the permanent endowment. In other words, depending upon the dollar threshold for a named endowment fund and how this is publicized (or not), prospects can either be attracted to contributing or dissuaded. If it is true, as so many people with whom I spoke contend, that contributors really do not care how their unrestricted deferred gifts are used by recipient institutions, maybe these policies do not matter. But maybe they do.

I have participated in numerous conversations about thresholds for an endowed fund especially one that is named or restricted for a purpose. The conundrum is based on the belief that if the entry level is too low, donors will direct current, unrestricted gifts away from the annual campaign toward endowment, and restricted contributions will have little or no impact on the organization and would entail more complexity in terms of accounting than they are worth. I have always argued that endowment funds are necessary and whatever policies attract donations should be encouraged, although I agree that designated funds should have a minimum gift requirement that is higher than that of an unrestricted contribution because they do take more effort to manage in relation to reporting and bookkeeping.

I have worked with organizations where the minimum for a named, unrestricted endowment fund is $1,000. These monies are pooled with all such funds for both investment and allocation purposes, and since they are therefore combined together, there is little extra work and much impact. Some organizations assign a much higher minimum gift level—even for an unrestricted fund—and universities and other large institutions have placed the entry level often at targets beyond the average donor's reach. This kind of policy might in fact deter gifts as opposed to encourage them. So, for example, when charities claim that unrestricted, realized gifts below a certain threshold are used upon receipt or placed into a board-restricted fund, and, more importantly, the donor's name is lost in the process, it seems that the policy does nothing to inspire future such gifts. Nor does it increase the endowment both at the time that the gift is realized and in terms of contributions precipitated by the marketing efforts that occur in a complementary fashion to receiving the donation. In other words, if part of endowment development is the marketing that accompanies a gift in order to inspire additional donors, it does not happen as a result of this process. Policies and marketing endowment building go "hand in hand."

Promotion is a key feature of any effort to encourage endowment gifts, and it, too, seems to be related, for the most part, to gift size. So, if minimum gift requirements are established and the ones at the lowest level are not publicly recognized, then the concept of establishing a threshold for endowment contributions does a disservice to the recipient organization if one of its goals is to increase the endowment. If describing gifts and donor stories are only limited to those with ever higher numbers, an opportunity for persuading others to make commitments might not result. In other words, if we impose minimum gift levels that also are related to donor recognition and only tell the stories of the largest gift givers and don't even identify those people who have contributed at lower levels, then we are negating the opportunity to both increase the endowment as well as provide the donor with the kind of satisfaction that such a contribution could afford.

Let me say this in a different way. Since the telling of donor stories is a constant among endowment programs, why are they limited to the biggest gifts? Why don't we include the names of all donors in marketing materials? Maybe the policy of the Combined Jewish Philanthropies in Boston is correct—any realized estate gift that is less than $1,000 will be used immediately; all others will be placed in the endowment and names of donors will be publicized in the annual report.[25] And another question: why do we limit the recognition that donors often want (implicitly if not explicitly) when they make an endowment contribution by only including the announcement of gifts of a certain size in our publications or on the web? In other words, in many cases minimum gift size for naming funds—whether restricted or otherwise—has more to do with management than development and may be impeding the latter.

One of the people whom I interviewed for this book and who preferred to remain anonymous told me that the organization for which he worked created several permanently endowed "impact" funds with broad parameters to which people were encouraged to contribute. For example, all donations dedicated to the domain of arts and culture would be placed in one fund. This is a common practice of educational institutions for scholarship monies or faculty support and of health-related organizations for research although these are often not permanent in nature, just restricted for a particular usage. This organization designed the areas of impact as expansively as possible and relating, quite appropriately, to its own current needs and future plans. In this way, the professional fundraiser explained to me, the charity would not have to deal with numerous restricted endowment accounts; the monies would be pooled for allocation to the impact area under which donor names would also be listed for the purpose of recognition. Of course gifts to the unrestricted endowment were the preference from the institution's perspective, but this new procedure provided for easier accounting and management of contributions while still allowing donors to express their preferences within the broad guidelines of the designated fields of interest. In addition the new framework was designed to limit the future obsolescence of named, restricted endowment funds and the legal complications that often result. On the other hand, this same individual cautioned me that I could not identify the organization because the board had yet to approve of the new arrangement. But at least the institution is doing what Doug White describes as "granularly" thinking about its policies in relation to raising endowment funds and recognizing donors.

There are many professionals who claim that it is too difficult to keep track of smaller funds or donors who make gifts of modest size, and I have often heard comments that "these are just not worth the effort." (Remember Simone Joyaux or think about that combined fundraising position—planned giving and major gift officer.) However, with all the technology that is available, this becomes a dubious argument. I can understand that distributions from restricted funds, in order to have any consequence in relation to an organization, need to be of a certain size. However, these contributions can, in turn, be combined by themes, subject matter, or general areas of concentration and allocations pooled to effect an impact on the recipient charitable institution.

The argument in this section is related to the concept of "institutional advancement" as opposed to appreciation of the donor and meaning of a gift. If we create policies to facilitate the management and marketing of the endowment that are coincident with the administrative needs of the organization, then we are in fact ignoring the donor and the kind of recognition that he or she may desire. Moreover, we are probably creating hurdles for supporters as opposed to encouraging endowment contributions. Marketing, policies, and donor recognition work together in a complementary fashion to ensure that the endowment-building function is encouraged and the future of the institution is therefore preserved.

I was surprised when I read a paragraph in Weinstein and Barden's book, *The Complete Guide to Fundraising Management*, in which the authors describe the importance of board support in establishing a new "planned giving" program. They list "a number of key decisions" that board members must make and include the following: "Should all undesignated bequests be used for operations? Or should the board place contributions over a certain amount in a board designated endowment fund?"[26] The authors offer no case for either choice nor mention that charities might want to differentiate between these options and the permanent endowment. They also do not explain how donors can ensure that their gifts are placed in the permanent endowment, what the advantages of doing so (or not) are, or how organizations can encourage them to make these contributions except to say that such a thing exists. There is no placement of the permanent endowment in a singular position of importance.

This model extends throughout their description of "planned gifts" in addition to the bequest. For example, when they describe charitable gift annuities, they include a representative agreement but also make no mention of the option of placing any remaining principal and income into the permanent endowment on the demise of the income beneficiary or beneficiaries. Instead they include the following wording: "The remainder shall be the property of the [Name of Organization] without any further claim or change thereon, to be used for the purpose of the corporation."[27] This is very different than the template of the United States Holocaust Museum as described in chapter 7 where the language clearly states that "upon termination of the charitable gift annuity, the remaining principal will be used to support the Museum's Permanent Endowment Fund or another specified purpose you may have designated."[28]

While this section of this chapter focuses on the interconnection between marketing and policies, mention must be made that there are numerous mechanisms for publicizing an endowment program just as there are many ways for an individual to create an endowment fund. The methods for promoting endowment giving and the policies for establishing endowments are not related. And while I am not going to describe all of the means available to encourage endowment contributions, I do suggest that they be identified in a strategic plan and include such items as newsletters, brochures, giving societies, videos, involvement in decision-making committees, and so on. What is important in terms of choosing and using these tools is to ensure that they encourage endowment giving and especially explain the differences in the eventual repository of a gift. It is also important that they communicate excellence in general and effective and trustworthy management in particular so that both a supporter and professional adviser can feel comfortable using a program in the case of the former and in recommending one in relation to the latter.

THE PROFESSIONAL ADVISER

I have often claimed that while it is important to be aware of some of the more complex gift mechanisms such as charitable remainder trusts and how they operate, these will most likely be brought to a not-for-profit organization by a donor's professional adviser. The issue for the institution is to guarantee that its endowment program is of such quality that these advisers will make referrals. No professional wants to be embarrassed by suggesting that a client donate to a not-for-profit that in turn "fumbles the pass."

I remember when a leader of an organization in which I worked congratulated me for procuring a multi-million-dollar charitable remainder trust. I replied that I had nothing to do with the actual gift; it was designed by the contributors' advisers, who did invite me to meet the donors when they were in the process of creating the trust. My only accomplishment was not losing the contribution to some other charity and convincing the donors that we would pay attention to them, personally, and manage their gift well. Ours was a new endowment initiative, but we included professional advisers at the very beginning of our planning and ensured that they knew what we were doing and how we were constructing our program. Our attention to them paid off not only with this gift, but so many more.

On this subject Weinstein and Barden agree that it is important to involve professional advisers in endowment building. They write that an organization's "executive director, development director, and key board members should network with estate-planning professionals: attorneys, certified public accountants, trust officers, insurance professionals, financial planners, and planned-giving advisers. These professionals should be told about the important work the organization does and be informed as to which types of planned gifts the charity accepts. Seek their advice and help."[29]

We always did just that. First, we appointed a well-known estate-planning attorney in town as the chairman of our board, and his successors, at least initially, also practiced in the same area of law. Their credibility and involvement signaled that we were a serious endeavor. We invited select professionals in the field to serve on the board, and all of these people were willing to refer clients to our program because they had a stake in its success and they had worked closely with us. We also created a professional advisory committee to consult with us in designing the initiative, and we coordinated with the local community foundation to promote educational seminars for all of the estate-planning professionals in the area. This was a cost-efficient method to bring to town well-known and expert speakers in the field, and these events were thus attractive to the professionals who attended the events in large numbers.

Weinstein and Barden write that "estate-planning professionals are among an organization's most important allies. Frequently they directly or indirectly offer recommendations when requested by philanthropic individuals who are making their estate plans. At a minimum, estate-planning professionals might ask whether clients have any interest in remembering any charitable organizations in a will or estate plan."[30] These professionals offer the equivalent of a "good housekeeping seal" to select endowment development programs, and therefore, especially on the local level, not-for-profit organizations must find a way to include them in their strategic marketing plans.

If an organization is relatively small and just starting a new endowment program, I usually recommend that it identify an attorney in the estate-planning field to advise it. (A community foundation can also serve this purpose.) This person may be a member of the board of the institution or not. More than one person might be invited to help whether the organization is national or local in scope. These professionals are essential to not only facilitate the launching of an effort; they also play an important role in reviewing documents, whether they be in relation to local regulations or created by donors' advisers. It is important that when an organization receives a contribution that has legal ramifications, for example, when the not-for-profit is named trustee of a charitable remainder trust or when a donor promises to provide funds over time to currently name a building or program, someone with the organization's interest examines the papers establishing the gift.

In large institutions, there is often a legal department that addresses these issues. In smaller charities, this is often not so, and thus a local professional must be engaged. However, like everything else, the organization first must develop guidelines in relation to how it will handle various donations, often referred to as "gift acceptance policies," and in my example above whether it will even serve as a trustee of a trust and if so, what kinds. Again, these are all policies that must be reviewed by a well-recognized professional adviser when establishing a program or at least during its initial period of operation, and several alternative perspectives should be sought and considered before a final determination is made by a board. Professional advisers are an essential part of this process.

NOTES

1. Eden Stiffman. "Setting Up a Planned Giving Program," *The Chronicle of Philanthropy*, February 27, 2015.
2. Stiffman, "Setting Up a Planned Giving Program."
3. Heather Joslyn, "A Planned-Giving 'Nirvana': How Big Investments in Fundraising for Bequests and Other Gifts Have Paid Off for the Nature Conservancy," *The Chronicle of Philanthropy*, October 2, 2018.
4. Stanley Weinstein and Pamela Barden, *The Complete Guide to Fundraising Management*, 4th ed. (Hoboken, NJ: John Wiley and Sons, 2017), 219–220.
5. Arlene D. Schiff, interview with author, November 21, 2019.

6. I wrote in chapter 4 that the importance of a culture of philanthropy as directed by the chief executive officer is essential. This was one of the primary findings of a study published in 2013 and commissioned by the Evelyn and Walter Haas Jr. Fund, *UnderDeveloped: A National Study of Challenges Facing Nonprofit Fundraising,* and it pertains here, too. The study "describes a culture of philanthropy as one in which 'most people in the organization (across positions) act as ambassadors and engage in relationship-building. Everyone promotes philanthropy and can articulate a case for giving. Fund development is viewed and valued as a mission-aligned program of the organization.'" In order for this perspective to work, the chief executive officer must be committed to this modus operandi and ensure that it happens.

7. Heather Joslyn, "It's All Hands on Deck to Seek Bequests," *The Chronicle of Philanthropy,* March 5, 2019.

8. Joslyn, "It's All Hands on Deck."

9. Scott C. Stevenson, "How to Start an Endowment for Your Nonprofit," *thebalancesmallbusiness,* September 16, 2019.

10. Stevenson, "How to Start an Endowment."

11. Douglas E. White, *The Art of Planned Giving* (New York: John Wiley and Sons, 1995), 226.

12. White, *The Art,* 236–239.

13. White, *The Art,* 237.

14. White, *The Art,* 237.

15. White, *The Art,* 238.

16. White, *The Art,* 238.

17. Anonymous, e-mail to Deborah Polivy, July 26, 2018. (I have chosen to not include the organization's name in this book in order to protect its anonymity.)

18. Deborah Kaplan Polivy, *Donor Cultivation and The Donor Lifecycle Map: A New Framework for Fundraising* (Hoboken, NJ: John Wiley and Sons, 2014), 88.

19. Joslyn, "A Planned-Giving 'Nirvana.'"

20. Joslyn, "A Planned-Giving 'Nirvana.'"

21. Stiffman, "Setting Up a Planned Giving Program."

22. Steven L. Meyers, *Personalized Philanthropy: Crash the Fundraising Matrix* (Nashville: CharityChannel Press, 2015), 110.

23. Joslyn, "It's All Hands on Deck."

24. Joslyn, "A Planned-Giving 'Nirvana.'"

25. Charles S. Glassenberg, e-mail to author, March 26, 2020. He wrote, "CJP [Combined Jewish Philanthropies] started formally recognizing our endowment donors each year in our Annual Report in 2008. We list all donors who give $1,000 or more, sorted by the fund they gave to, but not otherwise stratified by giving level. We include bequests to endowment in this list but annotate them with an '*' that keys to a footnote describing them as matured legacy gifts. Our web version omits the donor listings for privacy reasons."

26. Weinstein and Barden, *The Complete Guide,* 213.

27. Weinstein and Barden, *The Complete Guide,* 223.

28. https://www.ushmm.org/support/ways-to-give/planned-giving/options#Deferred%20Charitable%20Gift%20Annuity.

29. Weinstein and Barden, *The Complete Guide,* 214.

30. Weinstein and Barden, *The Complete Guide,* 215.

Chapter Nine

Conclusion

I attended a charity dinner a few weeks ago where the honorees made a witty and engaging speech that they ended by announcing that they had made a "legacy gift" for the benefit of the institution that had recognized them. That is all they said. I asked myself, what does that mean? What did they do? And even more importantly, why didn't they describe this "legacy gift" in order to inspire others who were present to think about the contribution and maybe consider something similar? This public statement, which was clearly meaningful to the honorees, seemed to have no impact on the audience. It may have been that the people who were listening just did not understand it.

Since I was writing this book at the time, I telephoned this couple to ask about the donation. They told me that they had made an arrangement with the local community foundation and their insurance agent. They purchased a policy on the life of the wife and donated it to the foundation that was then named both the owner and the beneficiary. The couple issued a check for the amount of the annual premium to the foundation, which then made the payment to the insurance company issuing the policy. This process would continue until the policy was fully paid. The couple would receive a charitable deduction on their federal income taxes for the amount of the premium payments. Weinstein and Barden describe this kind of contribution as follows: a donor can "purchase a life insurance policy on his or her life and irrevocably transfer its ownership to the charity." If a policy "continues to have annual premiums due, the donor can make a donation to the charity each year to cover the cost of the premium. He or she will receive an annual tax deduction for that donation."[1] In the case of these donors, the insurance was a whole life policy that would build cash value as premiums were paid.[2]

The couple also explained to me that they had instructed the foundation in writing that upon the wife's death, the proceeds from the policy should be used to establish three restricted, permanent endowment funds—one for each of two organizations in the community and the third for unrestricted grant making by the foundation itself. It was a nice gift, but no one in the audience on the night that they announced it realized its ultimate benefit.

Words do matter. In this case, the word "legacy" meant absolutely nothing to those present at the dinner. When these donors explained to me what they done, I thought to myself, "What a lost opportunity." If they had stated at the function that they had established three named endowment funds, including one for the organization that had honored them, and how they had done so, it might have had an extraordinary impact on the attendees. Some may have even thought about following suit or establishing an endowment fund using a different asset or mechanism. I was also a little bothered that none of the professional staff people involved with the gift—at the host organization itself or the community foundation—made any effort to encourage a more detailed description, although the couple did tell me that the foundation had asked them to announce the gift at its annual fundraising event. Hopefully, our conversation would inspire them to describe their contribution in more detail on that occasion.

There is another conclusion that can be drawn from this particular announcement. It, too, is related to language and marketing. If this same couple had stated that they had made a "planned gift," it probably would have been just as meaningless to the audience.

The words "legacy giving" are not any clearer than "planned giving" if no mention is made of permanence or endowment building. The gift made by this couple will in fact leave a legacy, but so many do not.

What is the point of legacy giving if there is in effect no legacy that is established in the end? If these gifts are just another label attached to a tool to raise more money, then why use the word "legacy"? And yet that is exactly the implication of the workshops offered on "Legacy Giving" at the "2020 Fund Raising Day in New York." The brochure advertising this event never once refers to "endowment development."[3]

"Legacy Giving" is one of the functional areas on which training is scheduled at this one-day conference along with "Advanced Fundraising," "Consulting," "Major Gifts," "Research & Prospect Development," and more. The presentations that are listed within the Legacy Giving rubric are all about how to "start" or "accelerate" a gift planning program or, if there is one in existence, to raise more money or work with the "Major Gift Officer or Planned Giving Officer." There is no mention of the purpose of the legacy gift or what is done with it once it is secured. In other words, notwithstanding that the workshops all fall under the title of "Legacy Giving," there is no mention of the endowment gift that would result if a legacy is in fact promised to the donor. In addition, and not surprisingly, there is a workshop entitled "It's Not Rocket Science: Understanding Planned Giving." And planned giving is linked with the major gift in order to "raise bigger gifts than you ever thought possible."[4]

Not only do words matter, but so do policies. Institutions need to review the way in which they market legacy giving and for that matter planned giving especially when they do not mention the word "endowment" in connection with these activities. Take a look at marketing brochures and websites of a variety of not-for-profit organizations. They are all about planned giving as opposed to the purpose of the planned gift.

Doug White encapsulates my argument quite concisely. He claims that a contribution, whether through planned giving, legacy giving, or what has now become gift planning, "is almost always marketed as a way to leave a legacy, which, if the money is spent right off, doesn't actually happen; so, the broader intent is not satisfied, even if the donor is unaware of the construct of the matter."[5] And he states that it is important to bring this issue "to the attention of the donor, and that it should be explicit that not only will the money be used in the category the donor wants, but that it will be used to create an endowed fund or put into an already existing one whose income is to be used for that purpose."[6]

What is especially worrisome is that White claims that many organizations, "not having thought it through, seem to blithely take the money and spend it all." He continues, "By the way, I feel the same about realized bequests; I know budgets are tight, but even without a gift agreement, it feels wrong to me to plop realized bequest proceeds into the operating budget because it's so up and down each year and charities, I strongly feel, need to budget against known expected income. As you say, they threaten their future health."[7]

I recommend that organizations think about how they are marketing and using so-called planned gifts, whether they are through bequests or any other gifting mechanism where the charity does not have access to the funds until some future time. Doug White agrees with me and writes, "Organizations need to give the process a lot more granular thought to this than most do. If they did, I imagine they would modify their by-laws in the way you describe."[8]

One of the people whom I interviewed and who asked to remain anonymous leads a planned giving department of a large, national organization. He told me that the board of this institution had discussed a policy on the disposition of "unrestricted, realized gifts," but that in "the absence of a resolution, these monies were primarily placed into a permanent, unrestricted endowment fund." He explained that some leaders "wanted to create a by-law" and formally direct such funds to the permanent endowment, but no consensus could be achieved. He did claim, however, that because of these discussions, increasingly conversations with donors were "more and more weighted toward endowment gifts."

So not only am I recommending changing the language—all the way down the line starting with the name of fundraising departments and including the titles of those who raise endowment monies—but also really discussing with decision makers including CEOs and boards how to market these donations and handle them when they are received. We should have in-depth or, as White suggests, "granular" conversations as to whether we are trying to build an endowment or not, and if the latter, stop telling supporters to leave a legacy when the organizations themselves are not treating the gifts in any kind of permanent, legacy-securing fashion. In other words, I suggest that not-for-profit organizations take a stand one way or another and decide whether to move forward with the Grinspoon Life & Legacy program model in which it is clearly stated that the goal is to raise endowment monies and then very simply describe how a donor can participate in the effort.[9] I also suggest that we remove all reference to planned giving because it is technical and, as White states, is somewhat "calcified"[10] at best.

The Harvard University website is very clear on this matter. It explains the options that a donor has "when making a bequest," which can be "unrestricted" and "left to the discretion of Harvard"; "restricted," which will support "ongoing specific University needs"; "endowed," which "provide[s] income every year in perpetuity to carry out the designated purpose of the gift, with the goal of preserving the real value of the gift"; or "expendable," where "the entire gift may be spent, generally within a relatively short time frame."[11] There is no mention of legacy giving or planned giving. On the other hand, there is also no mention of which model the university prefers nor the benefits of any of the gift types for the university or the donor. I think that not-for-profit organizations should provide these explanations to the prospect or donor so that he or she can make an educated choice when planning a gift that will be realized sometime in the future.

I have some additional recommendations in relation to the subject of endowment building. I think that fundraisers may be too cavalier when they claim that donors do not care how their unrestricted gifts are utilized. Or maybe they are correct. But unless we conduct some research in this area, we shall never really know. I therefore propose a study of a sample of people who say that they have left a gift to charity through an estate plan and ask them if they (1) know how the charities will use their respective gifts when they are eventually realized and (2) whether they in fact care. Is it these donors' assumption that the charities will use the monies on receipt for current needs or establish a permanent endowment fund bearing their name? A sample of respondents could be drawn from members of legacy societies representing different charities and areas of impact. In other words, do these people really not care as so many of my interviewees claim, or do they want to be permanently remembered as leaving a legacy behind either through a named endowment fund or at least a listing on a website or in an annual report? A national organization could fund such a study, and the results could erase some of the uncertainty around this issue. For example, if it is true that some donors give to endowment funds because they care about "the *sustainability* of [the] organization" (emphasis in the original), as claimed by the Fundraising Authority Team, and "they want to make sure that [the] non-profit, or at least one of its programs continues its work indefinitely,"[12] then not-for-profit organizations need to pay attention to what they do with these funds when they are received and even before in terms of how they publicize and explain donor options. If donors don't care, so be it, but charities cannot promise contributors a legacy if they are not in fact providing them with one.

Educating staff and board members on the subject of endowment development is another area that needs more work. We send people to conferences and expect them to return to our organizations as experts. Not so says Doug White in his book, *The Art of Planned Giving*.[13] We can give people some background so that when a donative opportunity appears, either directly from a contributor, for example, in the form of a charitable gift annuity or minimum retirement fund distribution, or through the offices of a professional adviser, they have a basic knowledge of the gifting mechanism and how it should be handled.

However, I have learned from my own experience that three things are necessary to make fundraisers competent endowment development professionals: ongoing training, experience with the actual gifts, and someone (or place) to call to request help when necessary. Sometimes these resources are one and the same and sometimes not. In any case, it seems to me that one of the roles of a community foundation is to provide expertise and counsel, especially to local not-for-profit organizations on the subject of endowment building.

A community foundation has an even broader responsibility if the Grinspoon Foundation Life & Legacy program is to serve as a prototype for an expansion that could have an extraordinary impact on the not-for-profit sector. I recommend that these foundations become proactive and, instead of providing one-time training to their respective community agencies in the form of workshops or other learning opportunities, they create and carry out an endowment-building program based on the Life & Legacy model.

Community foundations need to launch these programs by starting with the basics. They must educate their respective stakeholders about the importance of endowment building to the future sustainability of the not-for-profit sector in their geographic areas. And then they must more or less follow the steps of Life & Legacy by helping local organizations first identify their respective "loyal" donors, cultivate them, and then close gifts whether restricted for a particular organization or a number of them in which a prospect might be interested. These foundations must prepare training manuals as well as templates for advertisements, events, donor recognition, and conversations with prospects. The programs should include options for investing and managing the endowment funds that are raised for the benefit of the institutions that participate in the initiative. As a component part of the latter, there must be built-in coaching, just as in the Grinspoon model, so that the effort does not start and stop and continuity is assured. This element is especially important given that endowment building is an ongoing enterprise. A community foundation does not need to undertake the responsibility for such a program alone or underwrite the entire cost of the effort. But it can assume the role of "prime mover" in terms of launching it and mobilizing partners among private foundations and/or corporations to ensure the healthy future of the not-for-profit sector in which they all operate.

It is highly unlikely that individual local organizations, especially those without the infrastructure to pursue this kind of long-term fundraising, will embrace endowment development on their own, and there is every reason for funders to help ensure the future strength of these institutions. The community foundation, like the Grinspoon Foundation, can serve as a catalyst or convener of a local Life & Legacy initiative as opposed to waiting for agencies to individually request help in building their respective endowment funds—even if they could conceptualize such an effort given their concentration on annual fundraising. In the long run, such an initiative will strengthen each community for the benefit of all of its citizenry.

Endowment building over time has ensured that every generation is able to benefit from those that came before it. This process must continue onward. Doug White reminds us that "it is important to remember that endowments—at colleges, secondary schools, hospitals, or anywhere else—do not simply happen. In the vast majority of cases, they are the result of the efforts of past donors so possessed of a charitable commitment and of the financial ability to help preserve the charity's mission that they contributed to a cause they wished to see perpetuated."[14] However, in order to continue this dedication on the part of today's donors, organizational policies and procedures must encourage the process of endowment development—especially the permanent endowment. Investment has to be made in the endowment fundraising enterprise. This generation has the responsibility for those who come after it, and trustees of not-profit institutions must make those difficult decisions that balance today's needs and tomorrow's unknowns.

POSTSCRIPT

I wrote a large part of this manuscript while I was confined at home due to the 2020 coronavirus outbreak. That crisis confronted me with a challenge as well as frequent self-questioning. Maybe I was wrong. Given the very difficult circumstances that people found themselves in during the eruption of the virus, maybe endowment funds were not the answer that I thought they were in terms of protecting the future. Maybe the present was more important and current difficulties should be addressed with as much money as an organization had on hand—including realized, unrestricted contributions from estate gifts.

Then I remembered the e-mails that I received over time where charities were giving up on endowment development because of short-term financial challenges. I also recalled the article that I included in chapter 8 about the Nature Conservancy where an executive was quoted: "A lot of organizations cut back on planned-gift fundraising during tough economic times, preferring to focus on getting more dollars in the short term. 'The Nature Conservancy has never done that. . . . There's been a commitment toward [planned giving], and that has paid off.'"[15] And notwithstanding that I don't like the language of planned giving, I liked the attitude and the reminder that the Nature Conservancy was "a step ahead of most charities in preparing for the historic transfer of wealth that's starting to happen—and the opportunities it presents for fundraising."[16]

I had to keep reminding myself that we are only in a moment in time and that the future strength of the not-for-profit sector really did depend on endowment building and especially capturing both the current and upcoming wealth transfer in the process. And so while the crisis truly made me confront the implications of what I was writing, the research that I had completed and the e-mail messages that I had received reinforced my mission to not only change the language of endowment fundraising and to make it easier for all stakeholders to understand but also to encourage increased effort in this area in order to focus on the goal of securing the most money possible to ensure the future health of the third or what is better known as the not-for-profit sector. The need for endowment development has been proven time and again throughout this coronavirus pandemic. *The New York Times* stated the issue succinctly: "Institutions without a financial cushion will struggle to survive."[17]

NOTES

1. Stanley Weinstein and Pamela Barden, *The Complete Guide to Fundraising Management*, 4th ed. (Hoboken, NJ: John Wiley and Sons, 2017), 213.

2. It is interesting that several people who critiqued my manuscript had differing opinions about this gift. Some told me that they would never accept it: "Only the insurance agent would make money and the donors could stop paying the premiums." Another thought it was a fine gift. In any case, the only reason that I have included this anecdote is to demonstrate how language can be obfuscating.

3. Association of Fundraising Professionals New York City Chapter, "Moving Forward Together," Fund Raising Day in New York, Friday, June 5, 2020. (This occurred virtually because of the coronavirus outbreak.)

4. Association of Fundraising Professionals New York City Chapter, "Moving Forward Together," Fund Raising Day in New York, Friday, June 5, 2020.

5. Douglas E. White, e-mail to author, March 18, 2020.

6. Douglas E. White, e-mail to author, March 18, 2020.

7. Douglas E. White, e-mail to author, March 18, 2020.

8. Douglas E. White, e-mail to author, March 18, 2020.

9. Harold Grinspoon Foundation, The Life & Legacy Program, "Legacy Giving Options."

10. Douglas E. White, e-mail to author, March 18, 2010.

11. Harvard Alumni, "The Future Use of Your Bequest," https://alumni.harvard.edu/giving/bequests/future-use.

12. The Fundraising Authority Team, "What Motivates Endowment Donors to Give?" http://www.thefundraisingauthority.com/endowment-fundraising/motivating-endowment-donors/.

13. Douglas E. White, *The Art of Planned Giving* (New York: John Wiley and Sons, 1995), 302–303.

14. White, *The Art*, 13.

15. Heather Joslyn, "It's All Hands on Deck to Seek Bequests," *The Chronicle of Philanthropy*, March 5, 2019.

16. Joslyn, "It's All Hands on Deck."

17. Kevin Carey, "As States' Revenue Disappears, So Might the 'Public' in Public Colleges," *The New York Times*, May 7, 2020, A11.

Appendix A

The Life & Legacy Program Generic Letter of Intent

Community ABC
LETTER OF INTENT

In the tradition of our Jewish faith, I wish to share my blessings by declaring my intent to provide for the needs of future generations.

It is with deep satisfaction that:
____ I/We have already made a provision in my/our estate plan
____ I/We shall make a provision in my/our estate plan within the next ____ months *(12 months or less)*

I wish to support the following Community ABC institutions: (check all that apply)

____ Organization A	____ Organization F
____ Organization B	____ Organization G
____ Organization C	____ Organization H
____ Organization D	____ Other
____ Organization E	

With an endowment fund established through a:

____ Bequest in my will or trust	____ Life Insurance Policy
____ Remainder of IRA or other retirement plan	____ Charitable Remainder Trust
____ Gift of real estate, securities or other property	____ Donor-Advised Fund
____ Charitable Gift Annuity	____ Other _____
____ I wish to establish an endowment now with a current gift of cash or property	

Amount of Gift – Please choose one of the following two options:
____ The approximate value of my/our commitment will be $_____ or ___% of my/our estate/IRA/Insurance policy
____ I/we prefer to keep the details of this commitment confidential.

Privacy Statement: To encourage others to make commitments to the future, I/We permit my/our name(s) to be listed in printed materials and/or on our website:

____ I/We permit my name to be listed _____
____ I/We prefer to remain anonymous.   *(My name should appear as)*

Name(s): _____
Address: _____
City/State/Zip: _____
Phone: _____ **Email:** _____ **Birth date:** _____

I understand that this letter of intent is not a legal obligation and may be changed at my discretion at any time.

_____   _____
Signed   **Date**

_____   _____
Signed   **Date**

The Community ABC's professional staff can assist in creating endowed gifts. Please contact us with any questions or to establish your legacy. Together, we guarantee a Jewish tomorrow.

Community ABC
1234 Street
Town, State, Zip
Website
Contact person name, phone, email

***Source:* The Life & Legacy Program of the Harold Grinspoon Foundation**

Appendix B

The Life & Legacy Program Legacy Plan Guide

LEGACY PLAN GUIDE

The questions provided are intended to serve as a guide to help your Legacy Team discuss the different aspects of the plan and decide what will work for your specific organization.

Please put your legacy plan in narrative and/or bulleted format and submit as a Word document. Please do not just respond to the questions. Thank you!

Case Statement

Your case statement is different from most things you are asked to write. It is not a recruitment tool, but rather a reminder, to your most loyal donors, of the difference you make in their life and the life of your community. It focuses on the future and not on your current needs.

In addition to being the introduction to your Legacy plan, it is intended to be used as a stand-alone piece to share with the individuals you will be having legacy conversations with and to provide language for other marketing materials.

Please keep your case statement to one page, write in an *active tense*, and print in an easily readable font.

Your case statement should motivate and inspire members of your community to make a legacy commitment. It should be *positive, forward--looking* and *confident*. It should articulate why your organization must continue to flourish as an essential community resource now and for future generations.

Your case statement should describe the emotional connection donors have to your organization, focusing on **why** donors are devoted to you. It should invite donors to be part of your legacy society and clearly articulate the impact legacy gifts will have on those you serve.

Before you begin writing, we suggest that your legacy team share with each other why you have chosen to give your time, energy and financial resources to your organization and the important role it plays in your life. You may want to ask others involved with your organization these questions as well. These conversations will help you develop the appropriate language and feelings to convey in the case statement.

1

Source: **The Life & Legacy Program of the Harold Grinspoon Foundation**

Your case statement will have four parts:

1) Who you are and the role you play in the community
2) Your core values and how they are expressed
3) A statement that identifies who your legacy donors are i.e.: Our legacy donors are people just like you who believe/want....
4) Call to join/be part of this special group of people

To draft your case statement, consider the following questions:

- What impact has your organization had to date on you personally, in the community, the Jewish world and beyond (if applicable)?
- What are your organization's core values and what is the impact of these values on your constituents. How are they expressed?
- What is unique about what you provide/offer?
- What are your organization's future aspirations?
- What impact will legacy gifts have on those you serve?

When drafting your case statement make sure to:

- Write in active voice. You do not 'seek to educate' or 'hope to engage', etc.
- Use descriptive words to talk about the impact your organization has on its constituents.
- Share the values that motivate the organization's work.
- Shares the 'story' of your organization, why is your organization unique and needed in the community.
- Provoke the reader's emotions. Make them remember why the organization is special to them.
- Focus on what the organization has to offer future generations

Before submitting make sure you haven't:

- Presented a detailed history of your organization
- Talked about current or future needs
- Focused on how great your current staff is. The reader already knows!
- Overused words or abbreviations
- Focused on statistics such as how many people you have treated, how many religious school classes you have held or listed specific programs offered
- Written more than a page

Once submitted we will review your case statement, and the rest of your legacy plan, and offer suggestions to help make it as motivating a document as it can be so you start your legacy initiative with a strong foundation for success.

2

Source: **The Life & Legacy Program of the Harold Grinspoon Foundation**

Management Strategy

Your management strategy describes who is responsible for the implementation of your legacy efforts. It should clearly delineate who will have which responsibilities.

To draft your management strategy, **please list each legacy team member followed by their respective roles on the team.** Please note that saying "legacy team" is not sufficient:

- Which if not all, of your team members will be responsible for having conversations with donors?
- Who will be the lead person responsible for implementing the plan and keeping the team on track?
- Who will be responsible for tracking gifts, documents and records?
- Who will be responsible for submitting LIFE & LEGACY Quarterly reports and other required documentation?
- Who will be responsible for implementing your marketing plan? Who will be responsible for implementing your stewardship plan? Specifically who will be responsible for sending out the thank you notes, making sure thank you phone calls are made, making sure legacy events take place and that donor lists are printed?
- Who will be responsible for keeping your board of directors informed of your progress?

Target Audiences and Prospects

Your list of target audiences and prospects provides a listing of the categories of individuals you are planning to have legacy conversations with in the first two years, while building awareness of your legacy program among your entire constituency. **Please list these groups in priority order, starting with your Legacy Team**

To develop your target audience and prospect list, consider the following questions:

- Who is currently well informed about and well connected to your organization (i.e. board members, long-time donors)?
- Who are your long-time loyal and steady donors? (I.e. former board members, past presidents, those who have given a specific amount to annual campaigns for 10 years or more, longtime members, and longtime volunteers)?
- Who are currently receiving services at a meaningful point in their lives (residents of senior living facilities, B'nai Mitzvah families, families whose children are receiving camp scholarships or other financial assistance)?
- Others who have warm feelings for your organization (volunteers, alumni, founders)?

3

Source: The Life & Legacy Program of the Harold Grinspoon Foundation

- Considering the longer term, which of your constituents are of an age where they are thinking about wills and estate planning (generally 40's and older)?
- Groups to whom you can make a presentation and then follow-up with individual conversations?
    o   Your board
    o   Sisterhood or Men's Club
    o   Minyanaires
    o   Hebrew School families
    o   Past presidents

Marketing

During the LIFE & LEGACY training process you will receive information on how to market your Legacy program. As part of your Legacy Plan we want you to begin thinking of ways you can "get the message out," given your current organizational infrastructure.

To draft your marketing plan, consider the following questions:

- Which communication vehicles are currently in place and could be used for marketing your Legacy program?
    o   Newsletter – articles/ads
    o   Weekly announcements at services/meetings/via email
    o   Website
    o   Posters / video board / flyers
    o   Events
    o   Direct mail
    o   Blast emails
    o   Social media
- How can each of them be used to spread the Legacy message --- and how often?
- Is there a visible physical location to post information about leaving a Legacy or to honor those who do?
- Is there someone in your organization who can interview legacy donors and either write up or tape video testimonials to be shared with others in your community?
- Is it feasible to add some legacy information, at no additional cost, to one or more already scheduled mailings? *Creates awareness but doesn't result in significant number of commitments.*
- Is it feasible to print a separate legacy focused brochure or to incorporate a legacy message into an existing informational piece?
- Are there annual gatherings or other events into which a legacy message can be incorporated?
- Can you easily incorporate legacy information into your existing website?

4

Source: The Life & Legacy Program of the Harold Grinspoon Foundation

- If you use social media, can you intersperse a few legacy-themed messages into your usual postings?

Stewardship

Stewardship is key to the success of any Legacy program as it is the way we show appreciation to, and stay connected with, those who have made a legacy commitment. During the LIFE & LEGACY training process we will share stewardship best practices. As part of your Legacy Plan, we want you to begin to think about methods you can easily implement to acknowledge legacy commitments. Best practices include acknowledging, recognizing and engaging your legacy donors a minimum of four times a year.

To draft your stewardship/recognition plan, consider the following questions:

- What types of stewardship activities is your organization currently engaged in?
- Is it possible to include your legacy donors in these existing stewardship activities?
- What types of stewardship activities, if any, will you undertake specifically for legacy donors?
- Will you make a personal phone call immediately upon receipt of a Letter of Intent?
- Will you send a personal note thanking the donor for their Legacy commitment within two days of receipt?
- Will you create a legacy society or incorporate LIFE & LEGACY donors into an existing legacy giving initiative? Will you list legacy society members in a newsletter or acknowledge commitments somewhere in your building?
- Will you send cards at birthdays, Rosh Hashanah, Hanukkah, and/or Passover?
- Will you send a card on the anniversary of your legacy donor's commitment?
- Will you send an organizational update specifically for Legacy donors at least once a year?
- Will you host an event for Legacy donors either stand-alone or as part of (before or after) another organizational event?
- Will you honor Legacy donors at an annual/congregational meeting?
- Will you share testimonials from your Legacy donors with the greater community?

Goals

Participation in the LIFE & LEGACY program requires the establishment of goals for Letters of Intent to be secured each year for a period of two years.

The minimum goal per organization per year is 18 Legacy commitments although we encourage organizations to aspire to secure 25 commitments per year as in the long run this will be of greater benefit to your organization.

5

Source: **The Life & Legacy Program of the Harold Grinspoon Foundation**

For each year please note the number of letters of intent you are committed to securing. **Please note that whatever number you include in your plan is the goal you need to reach to secure the incentive grant.**

You can just articulate your goal in a sentence or you can be more specific as shown in this example:

Year 1	# of Legacy gifts
Legacy team members	4
Board of Directors (20 people)	10
Long-time Donors (any level)	3
Past Presidents	1
Total anticipated gifts in Year 1	**18**

Year 2	# of Legacy gifts
Board of Directors (20 people)	5
Long-time Donors (any level)	7
Past Presidents	3
Capital Campaign contributors	3
Total anticipated gifts in Year 2	**18**

Implementation Checklist

This final section of your Legacy Plan is a checklist of tasks to be accomplished in Year 1. The more specific you can be, the better as this list will assist you in staying on track and reaching your goal. **All activities mentioned under management, target audiences and prospects, marketing, stewardship and goals should be included as either a bulleted set of to-do-items that can be checked off or a calendar highlighting when you are going to undertake each activity.** To assure greater accountability also list the individual responsible for accomplishing the task.

We look forward to reviewing your plan with you!

Revised September 2016

6

Source: The Life & Legacy Program of the Harold Grinspoon Foundation

Appendix C

The Life & Legacy Program Partnership Agreement

(Jewish Federation/Foundation of XXX)
LIFE & LEGACY™ Partnership Agreement

(Name of your organization) _____ and the (Federation/Foundation) shall:
- commit to working together on this four-year program
- treat each other and donors with the utmost respect
- consider the well-being and interests of the donors first
- be confidential and not participate in *Lashon Hara* (evil speech)
- be good listeners, responsive and inclusive
- recognize the importance of *Ahavat Israel* (the love of the Jewish community) and strive for the betterment of the entire community

(Name of your organization) _____ shall:
- form a legacy team consisting of at least one professional and a minimum of three key lay leaders
- attend all LIFE & LEGACY workshops/trainings/meetings
- draft a legacy plan and meet with HGF staff to discuss
- finalize the legacy plan and submit to legacy coordinator
- be timely and responsive to communication and information requests, including quarterly reports
- secure legacy commitments to meet incentive grant goals and implement stewardship best practices
- meet with Federation/Foundation and HGF staff to share progress, successes and/or challenges
- share the names of donors who have given permission with the Federation/Foundation
- incorporate the LIFE & LEGACY logo and messaging into the organization's marketing
- submit "Letters of Intent" for verification purposes
  (the remaining bullets in this section are optional based on your Federation/Foundation's requirements)
- establish an endowment fund with the Federation/Foundation (if not already established), and place all bequests and other planned gifts obtained through the LIFE & LEGACY program into this fund
- share with federation/foundation a list of first 20 prospects, for the purpose of evaluating overlap with other organizations
- establish board-approved written endowment policies and procedures

(Name of Federation/Foundation) shall, in collaboration with HGF:
- implement the LIFE & LEGACY program locally, secure funding and select participating organizations
- provide incentive grants each year for four years to organizations reaching defined measurable goals
- offer high quality group and individual training seminars
- guide each organization in developing a legacy plan, implementing action and tracking progress
- provide consulting and coaching services including technical assistance related to formalization of legacy commitments
- implement a community-wide marketing plan and provide marketing assistance to partners
- maintain confidentiality of your financial information and respect the wishes of donors who choose anonymity.

_____   _____
Organization Representative/President   Federation/Foundation

_____
Synagogue Rabbi/Clergy/Executive Director

Date_____   Date_____

Source: The Life & Legacy Program of the Harold Grinspoon Foundation

Index

128   *Index*

About the Author

Deborah Kaplan Polivy, PhD, wrote *The Donor Lifecycle Map: A Model for Fundraising Success* (2017), which built on the ideas presented in her first book, *Donor Cultivation and the Donor Lifecycle Map: A New Framework for Fundraising* (2014). She began her professional career at Allied Jewish Community Services in Montreal, Quebec, and then helped to establish two successful Jewish Federation foundations. Deborah also served as the director of total financial resource development for the Jewish Federation of Greater New Haven. She was the director of development for Goodspeed Musicals, the originator of the musical *Annie*, where she managed the initial stages of a capital campaign for a new theater.

Deborah has served as a research associate at Yale University's Program on Nonprofit Organizations, where she conducted studies on the United Way and corporate charitable payroll deduction programs. She has taught at McGill and Brandeis Universities and Smith and Trinity (Hartford, Connecticut) Colleges, and as a consultant, she has trained staff and volunteers on fundraising with a specialty on endowment building. Her doctoral degree is from the Heller School for Social Policy and Management at Brandeis University, where she is a proud member of the board of advisors. Her website is http://www.deborahpolivy.com.